First World War
and Army of Occupation
War Diary
France, Belgium and Germany

21 DIVISION
110 Infantry Brigade
Leicestershire Regiment
9th Battalion
1 July 1916 - 20 February 1918

WO95/2165/2

The Naval & Military Press Ltd
www.nmarchive.com
Published in association with The National Archives

Published by

The Naval & Military Press Ltd

Unit 10 Ridgewood Industrial Park,

Uckfield, East Sussex,

TN22 5QE England

Tel: +44 (0) 1825 749494

www.naval-military-press.com

www.nmarchive.com

This diary has been reprinted in facsimile from the original. Any imperfections are inevitably reproduced and the quality may fall short of modern type and cartographic standards.

© **Crown Copyright**
Images reproduced by permission of The National Archives, London, England, 2015.

Contents

Document type	Place/Title	Date From	Date To
Heading	WO95/2165/2		
Miscellaneous	21st Division 110th Infy Bde 9th Bn Leicesters. Regt Jly 1916-Feb 1918		
Heading	110th Inf. Bde. 21st Div. Battn. transferred With Bde. from 37th Div. 7.7.16. War Diary. 9th Battn. The Leicestershire Regiment. July 1916 Jeb 18		
War Diary		01/07/1916	10/07/1916
War Diary		01/07/1916	31/07/1916
Heading	110th Brigade. 21st Division. 1/9th Battalion Leicestershire Regiment August 1916		
War Diary	Trenches Arras	01/08/1916	07/08/1916
War Diary	Billets in Arras	08/08/1916	18/08/1916
War Diary	Trenches Arras	19/08/1916	31/08/1916
Heading	110th Brigade 21st Division. 1/9th Battalion Leicestershire Regiment September 1916		
War Diary	Trenches Arras	01/09/1916	18/09/1916
War Diary	Bivouac	19/09/1916	19/09/1916
War Diary	Near Bernafay	20/09/1916	20/09/1916
Miscellaneous	Wood	21/09/1916	23/09/1916
War Diary	Assembly Trenches	24/09/1916	27/09/1916
Miscellaneous	A Form Messages And Signals.		
War Diary		02/10/1916	31/10/1916
War Diary	Front Trenches	01/11/1916	01/11/1916
War Diary	Hohenzollern Sector	02/11/1916	02/11/1916
War Diary	Support Trenches	03/11/1916	08/11/1916
War Diary	Front Trenches	09/11/1916	15/11/1916
War Diary	Reserve Trenches	16/11/1916	20/11/1916
War Diary	Front	21/11/1916	21/11/1916
War Diary	Line	22/11/1916	22/11/1916
War Diary	Trenches	23/11/1916	30/11/1916
War Diary	Support Trenches	01/12/1916	03/12/1916
War Diary	Front Trenches	04/12/1916	09/12/1916
War Diary	Reserve	10/12/1916	15/12/1916
War Diary	Bethune	16/12/1916	24/12/1916
War Diary	Raimbert	25/12/1916	31/12/1916
War Diary	Billets Raimbert	01/01/1917	28/01/1917
Miscellaneous	Billets	29/01/1917	31/01/1917
War Diary	Billets Houterque Area	01/02/1917	14/02/1917
War Diary	Trenches Hohenzollern	15/02/1917	28/02/1917
War Diary	Trenches Hohenzollern Sector	01/03/1917	27/03/1917
War Diary	Billets Sailly	28/03/1917	29/03/1917
War Diary	Billets Gaudismare	30/03/1917	31/03/1917
War Diary	Gaudiempre	01/04/1917	02/04/1917
War Diary	Pommier	03/04/1917	03/04/1917
War Diary	Moyenneville	05/04/1917	06/04/1917
War Diary	Outpost Line Croiselles	07/04/1917	15/04/1917
War Diary	Bailleulval	16/04/1917	22/04/1917
War Diary	Ayette	23/04/1917	24/04/1917
War Diary	Hamelincourt	25/04/1917	28/04/1917
War Diary	Boiry Becquerelle	29/04/1917	31/05/1917

Map	Cherisy. Detail and Trenches revised to 30-5-17		
War Diary	Pommier	01/06/1917	01/06/1917
War Diary	Moyenneville	02/06/1917	06/06/1917
War Diary	Trenches	07/06/1917	30/06/1917
Map	Fontaine-Lez-Croisilles		
War Diary		01/07/1917	31/07/1917
War Diary	Moyenneville	01/08/1917	08/08/1917
War Diary	Croisilles Trenches	08/08/1917	17/08/1917
War Diary	Ervillers	18/08/1917	24/08/1917
War Diary	Gouy-En-Artois	25/08/1917	25/08/1917
War Diary	Izel Lez Hameau	26/08/1917	31/08/1917
Map	Scale 1:10000-Fontaine No. 2		
Map	3rd Field Survey Coy R.E. (1395)		
War Diary	Izel Lez Hameau	01/09/1917	14/09/1917
War Diary	Crestre	15/09/1917	20/09/1917
War Diary	Meteren	23/09/1917	25/09/1917
War Diary	La Clytte Hallabest	26/09/1917	30/09/1917
War Diary	Trenches in Front of Polycon Wood J. 16 a. 7.9 to J. 10. E. 7.6	01/10/1917	20/02/1918

WO 95/21652

21ST DIVISION
110TH INFY BDE

9TH BN LEICESTERS. REGT

JLY 1916 — FEB 1918

Joined 37 Div

Disbanded 7/2/18

21ST DIVISION
110TH INFY BDE

MAPS & PLANS
RECORDED

110th Inf.Bde.
21st Div.

Battn. transferred
with Bde. from
37th Div. 7.7.16.

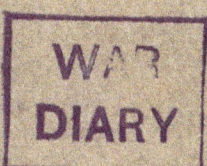

9th BATTN. THE LEICESTERSHIRE REGIMENT.

J U L Y

1916

Feb. '18

Confidential.

Subject: War Diary

INTELLIGENCE SUMMARY

To: D.A.A. & Q.M.G.
21st Division.

From: O.C. 9th Leicestershire Regt.

Herewith War Diary of
9th (Serv) Battn. The Leicestershire Regt
for month of July 1916, as per
your C/1157 of 19/7/16.

C.H. Haig Lt. Colonel.
Commdg. 9th Leicestershire Regt.

1/8/16.

INTELLIGENCE SUMMARY.

(Erase heading not required.)

Place	Date	Hour	Summary of Events and Information	Remarks and references to Appendices
	July 1st		The Battn. moved to SOUASTRE via LAHERLIERE – LA BAZEQUE FARM – ST. AMAND.	
	2nd.		The Battn. was in readiness to reinforce 46th. or 56th. Divisions who were attacking at GOMMECOURT. At 10.30 p.m. Battn. received orders to be ready to move early on 2nd to HEBUTERNE. Battn. was now attached to the 56th. Division. Battn. still stood by ready to move off but received orders at 9.55 p.m. to march back to HUMBERCAMP on the 3rd.	
	3rd.		The Battn. marched to HUMBERCAMP via ST AMAND. Day passed quietly.	
	4th/5th 6th.		Battn. carried on training and were in readiness to move at short notice. Battn. moved to TALMAS by route march via PAS – MARIEUX – PUCHEVILLERS. Starting at 4 p.m. and arriving at 10.20 p.m.	
	7th.		Battn. moved again by route march to CROUY en NAOURS – WARGNIES – WARGNIECOURT – BOURDON starting at 9 a.m. and arrived at 5.15 p.m.	
	8th.		Battn. rest'd. All inspections were carried out.	
	9th.		The Divl. Commander addressed all officers on the coming offensive and action. Battn. moved off from CROUY at 2.30 a.m. by rail to AILLY-sur-SOMME and thence railed to MERICOURT – l'Abbé by bus to MEALTE where it bivouacked.	

WAR DIARY
or
INTELLIGENCE SUMMARY.
(Erase heading not required.)

Army Form C. 2118.

Place	Date	Hour	Summary of Events and Information	Remarks and references to Appendices
	10th contd.		until 9pm. – At that hour moved to FRICOURT – at 11.30p.m. took over QUADRANGLE TRENCH and QUADRANGLE SUPPORT (which had previously been captured by 10th Brigade) – 1 Coy Q. SUPPORT, 1 Coy PEARL ALLEY – 2 Coys Q. TRENCH – Relief completed 4 a.m.	
	11th	11h.	Heavy shelling all 11th but no infantry attack. MAJOR A.W.L. TROTTER and 2 Lieut. A.B. TAYLOR killed } SHELL FIRE 2/Lieut. H.F. KING. wounded }	
	12th.		C Coy. relieved D in Q. SUPPORT. B Coy relieved by 8/R BERKS. in PEARL ALLEY and moved back to FRICOURT Bath. relieved by 10th K.O.Y.L.I. and moved back to FRICOURT arriving back about 5am. 13th. Casualties 10–13th. 3 Offrs. + 30 O.R.	
	12th–13th			
	13th.		12 Offrs. and 600 men employed from 9am to 6pm carrying up wire ammunition and grenades to MAMETZ WOOD. 2 Brigade Conferences as to orders for Brigade to attack BAZENTIN–LE–PETIT WOOD. [Order cancelled] Bath. moved off at 12.15am and moved up to S. edge of MAMETZ WOOD. Heavy shelling – Reached Reserve position MAMETZ WOOD 500 yds. W. of front Edge at 3.20 a.m. Just as intense bombardment of German trenches began	
	14th			

Place	Date	Hour	Summary of Events and Information	Remarks and references to Appendices
	14th Contd		and other went into existing trenches & dug in	
		5.30am	B Coy (Capt Andrew) and 1 Platoon of A moved over to BAZENTIN-LE-PETIT Wood to reinforce 6th Bn. — They finally reached N. of wood of village and as far as possible dug themselves in — They were mixed up with 6,7, & 8th Bns. Many casualties including all Coy officers. At 6am remainder of A Coy moved to German front line trench and started to consolidate it — 2 Platoons C Coy taken to Bde. H.Q. for carrying. At 8.15am Lieut Col. HAIG with D and ½ C moved to BAZENTIN-LE-PETIT Wood. Lt. Col. HAIG had orders to take over defence of N.W. and W. edges of wood which were being heavily shelled.	
		8.45am	D Coy (Lieut. Nolan) directed on N.W. corner of wood to clear wood and dig in on edge. 2 Platoons C Coy in support. Trench with Bn. H.Q.	
		9am–12noon	D Coy met with heavy opposition and reached forward support line but failed to clear wood. Lieut. Nolan killed, Lt. de Trafa and Smith wounded.	
		12noon–3pm	Germans threatened counter attack — Very heavy shelling of all lines. A Coy brought to Bn. H.Q. and 2 platoons sent to reinforce 6th Bn.	

Army Form C. 2118.

WAR DIARY
or
INTELLIGENCE SUMMARY.
(Erase heading not required.)

Place	Date	Hour	Summary of Events and Information	Remarks and references to Appendices
14th contd. (12noon)			Col. Kumme 2 Lt. + 30 men captured by D Coy. Capt. Bowler (A) Badly wounded.	
		4pm-7pm	Brigadier came out and ordered all available men to attack N.W. edge of wood. Lt. Col. Haig, Capt. Emmett and Lieut. Stephens not about 50 men returned reporting in about 100 men of 10th E. Yorks as supports. Capt. Emmett with 40 men reached N.W. edge of wood and killed & German sentries and attempted to charge German trench 50 yds from edge of wood. Capt. Emmett & 20 men killed by M.G. fire. Meanwhile Lt. Col. Haig with 1st & 6 Yorks and refs of 9th had reached Railway line and came under enfilade M.G. fire (Lt. Stephens killed). The edge of wood close to village were silenced and a small force organized towards Capt Emmetts party — they came under heavy enfilade fire and just finally. No reinforcement met arriving the men billed or wounded. All posts started consolidating when big guns Capts sent out constantly from the clearing post. Regt. available as set below.	Shewn below held by no.
		7pm		

Army Form C. 2118.

WAR DIARY
or
INTELLIGENCE SUMMARY.
(Erase heading not required.)

Instructions regarding War Diaries and Intelligence Summaries are contained in F. S. Regs., Part II. and the Staff Manual respectively. Title pages will be prepared in manuscript.

Place	Date	Hour	Summary of Events and Information	Remarks and references to Appendices
H.K. Smith		9pm–11pm	Heavy shelling and enemy rifle fire but no actual organised attack.	
15K.		2am.	Batt. ordered to go back to outskirts of MAMETZ wood by 5am.	
		5am.	Arrived at rendezvous.	
		9am.	Ordered to return to original posts.	
		9.45am	Reached original line with slight losses. The day was spent in clearing the wood and reorganising Coys.	
16K.			Same as preceding days. Rations carried up but had not done before and now got food and rum and became a little less exhausted.	
15K.		9pm	2/Lt. Sargent and 20 men went to dig trenches in a N.W. edge of wood. They arrived at position but were noticed with a Barrage of Rifle, Grenades schrap stein and are believed to have been all killed or wounded.	
16K.		3pm.	2/Lt. Rice and 1 Platoon sent to forward Railway line behind 2/Lt. Sargent in support of the Yorks. They endeavoured to find 2/Lt. Sargent's party but failed.	
		5.30pm.	Major Bent with D + B Coys went to BAZENTIN-LE-PETIT village. 2 Coys 9/K. R. Coy. Batt.	

Army Form C. 2118.

Instructions regarding War Diaries and Intelligence Summaries are contained in F.S. Regs., Part II. and the Staff Manual respectively. Title pages will be prepared in manuscript.

WAR DIARY
or
INTELLIGENCE SUMMARY.
(Erase heading not required.)

Place	Date	Hour	Summary of Events and Information	Remarks and references to Appendices
16K.(nth	16th	9pm	Orders received that we would be relieved by 64th Inf Bde - Relief was very slow owing to the great passing up of units.	
	16-17th		Last party relieved and reached Bivouac near FRICOURT at noon 17th inst.	
	17th	7.30pm	Bathed in Bathes during journey 14-17th July 18 off. 390 O.R.	
	18th 19th		Batts & Transport marched to RIBEMONT arriving 1am 18th	
	20th		Cleaned and rested	
			Batts entrained at 12 noon from MERICOURT to SALEUX (Transport by Road) Arrived SALEUX 7pm and marched to CROUY. Arrived there 12.15am 20th	
21st	9.30pm		Cleaned and rested. Moved by motor lorry (Transport by Road) to LONGPRÉ (Bivouac) Last party arrived 2am. 22nd.	
	22nd	4pm	Moved to LONGEAU and entrained 7pm for St. Pol reaching there 2am 23rd. A Coy unloaded LONGEAU Baggage fatigue	
	23rd	2am	Marched to Rest Camp.	
		10.30am	Marched to COUY-EN-TERNOIS	
	24th	5.30am	Cleaned and rested. A Coy rejoined Battn.	

WAR DIARY
or
INTELLIGENCE SUMMARY.

(Erase heading not required.)

Army Form C. 2118.

Place	Date	Hour	Summary of Events and Information	Remarks and references to Appendices
	25th		The Battn. moved to LATTRE-ST.-QUENTIN by motor lorry at 6pm.	
	26th		Battn. rested. C.O. and Company Commanders went to inspect trenches in J.2. ARRAS Sector.	
	27th		Battn. moved to ARRAS leaving LATTRE at 1.35 p.m. halting at MANQUEVIN until 7.30 p.m. Arrived ARRAS 11 p.m. Battn. sent into billets in ARRAS.	
	28th		At 4 p.m. Battn. moved from billets and took over trenches 93-97 J.2. ARRAS Sector from 6th D.C.L.I. 2 Companies front line, 2 Companies Support. Relief completed by 6.55 p.m.	
	29th, 30th, & 31st		No incident of importance. Work of consolidation of craters and defence line carried on. Enemy particularly inactive.	

1-8-16.

C. H. Herts. Lieut-Colonel. Commdg.
9th (Ser) Battn. the Leicestershire Regt.

110th Brigade.

21st Division.

1/9th BATTALION

LEICESTERSHIRE REGIMENT

AUGUST 1916.

Army Form C. 2118

WAR DIARY
or
INTELLIGENCE SUMMARY.
(Erase heading not required.)

9 Leicesters

Place	Date	Hour	Summary of Events and Information	Remarks and references to Appendices
Trenches ARRAS.	Aug 1st – 4th		Enemy very inactive. Days passed quietly. The trenches need considerable work. They are very shallow and bad.	
	Aug 5th		Considerable aeroplane activity especially on our part. The enemy fired about 20 rounds into and behind trenches 96 + 97.	
	Aug 6th		At 12.4 p.m. the enemy suddenly opened an intense bombardment for 15 minutes but made no attempt to enter our trenches. The trenches were badly damaged. Casualties were very slight. 1 killed 2 wounded. It is reported that the enemy attempted a raid on our left which failed.	
	Aug 7th		No Activity. The Battn. was relieved by 7th Battn. in the evening. Relief complete by 12.15 am. Casualties nil. Battn. marched back to billets in ARRAS.	
BILLETS in ARRAS.	Aug 8th. – 9th		After cleaning up. Battn. found 356. O.R. for working parties. The trenches were not shelled but about 6 pm by enemy artillery fire. Considerable shelling of vicinity followed.	
	Aug 10 – 17th		Battn. found 356 men for work parties on trenches, principally making dugouts and carrying for R.E. On night of Aug 14 – 15th the enemy flung 2 mine in front of 95 trench but failed to penetrate on lines.	

Army Form C. 2118.

WAR DIARY
or
INTELLIGENCE SUMMARY.
(Erase heading not required.)

Instructions regarding War Diaries and Intelligence Summaries are contained in F.S. Regs., Part II. and the Staff Manual respectively. Title pages will be prepared in manuscript.

Place	Date	Hour	Summary of Events and Information	Remarks and references to Appendices
	Aug. 18th		1st Batt. relieved the 12th N.F.'s in trenches 81-88. Relief complete by 12 noon without casualties. Trenches taken over from R. Scarpe on South to G.17.d.10.10.16 G.11.d.9.a. Sheet 51.B.N.W.1.	
Tranches ARRAS.	Aug. 19th		Enemy very quiet. Our get on with trench work. Much bombing and rooting. Our patrol saw large enemy working party. A Lewis Gun was brought into action and dispersed it.	
	Aug. 20th		Very little activity of any kind. Trench Mortars turn 30 shells over doing a little damage but nothing else.	
	Aug. 21st		Enemy aeroplane flew over at 3.30 p.m. Our strongpoint and wiring. Our patrols encountered none of the enemy.	
	Aug. 22nd		Enemy trench mortars active. Considerable damage done to trenches but no casualties. Enemy again on trenches with 105 m.m. shells. Enemy again were in front of Bn. They were dispersed by our Field Gun Fire. Our trench mortars retaliated on German lines.	
	Aug. 23rd		Trench Mortars again caused us trouble. Rifle Grenades and aerial torpedoes were also sent over. Little damage. Enemy snipers more active. No one hit. Patrol immediately in front of our own looking over.	
	Aug. 24th		An Officer wearing grey cap with black patent leather peak was seen looking over barricade. He was fired at and did not appear again. Strengthening our wire in front of Rooon. Sap. Enemy very quiet.	

T2134. Wt. W708—776. 500000. 4/16. Sir J.C. & B.

Army Form C. 2118.

WAR DIARY
or
INTELLIGENCE SUMMARY.
(Erase heading not required.)

Instructions regarding War Diaries and Intelligence Summaries are contained in F. S. Regs., Part II. and the Staff Manual respectively. Title pages will be prepared in manuscript.

Place	Date	Hour	Summary of Events and Information	Remarks and references to Appendices
	Aug. 25th		Enemy's trench mortars fired 20 shots into our support, knocking in 3. Damage done to trenches very little. Our Lewis Guns dispersed an enemy working party at 3:10 a.m. Our patrol did not see anything of the enemy.	
	Aug. 26th		No activity on trench mortar activity. Enemy officer and others shot about 20 bombs into "No Man's Land" from his hammock.	
	Aug. 27th		Enemy two men strengthening his advanced post. Our patrol was out from 10.30 p.m. till 12.15 a.m. but encountered none of the enemy.	
	Aug. 28th		Enemy trench mortars active. Considerable damage done to MARCH AVENUE also FEBRUARY AVENUE. Small avoids for one or two lines in a distance of 50/60ft from EAST to WEST making a bad scene. Two patrols sent out. Neither encountering any of the enemy. Our trench mortars bombarded enemy front line doing a good deal of damage to his wire.	
	Aug. 29th		Our trench mortars cut enemy wire. Our patrol went out to watch if enemy was doing anything. If they came out to wire, our patrol was to fire. The Lewis Guns are to control.	
	Aug. 30th			
	Aug. 31st		Our patrol sent out with the same idea as yesterday. The time he swung.	

Army Form C. 2118.

WAR DIARY
or
INTELLIGENCE SUMMARY.
(Erase heading not required.)

Instructions regarding War Diaries and Intelligence Summaries are contained in F. S. Regs., Part II. and the Staff Manual respectively. Title pages will be prepared in manuscript.

Place	Date	Hour	Summary of Events and Information	Remarks and references to Appendices
MAY AVENUE.	Aug 31st (cont)		enemy party did come out and our artillery opened fire and dispersed them. It is not known what casualties we caused. Trench mortars did considerable damage to	
			Casualties during Month:- Officers NIL. O.R. Killed 3. Wounded 18.	
	1-9-16			

Offley Lieut Colonel.
Commdg. 9th (Sev) Batt. The Leicestershire Regt.

110th Brigade.
21st Division.

1/9th BATTALION

LEICESTERSHIRE REGIMENT

SEPTEMBER 1916.

WAR DIARY or INTELLIGENCE SUMMARY

Army Form C. 2118

Sept 1st to December 9th 1914 Vol 15

14.C.
19 Mid[?]

Place	Date	Hour	Summary of Events and Information	Remarks and references to Appendices
Trenches ARRAS	Sept 1st to Sept 2nd Sept 3rd		Days passed quietly. Enemy fired mortars fired occasionally. Batt. was relieved by 16th Batt. Cheshire Regt. Relief carried out successfully without casualties. Batt. marched back to AGNEZ-le-DUISONS where it billeted for the night.	
	Sept 4th Sept 5th Sept 6th to Sept 12th Sept 13th Sept 14th		Batt. left AGNEZ le DUISONS at 7 a.m. & marched to MAGNICOURT. Day spent cleaning up and re-equipping. Days spent in hard training - route marches - physical drill - bayonet fighting etc. Batt. marched to FREVENT, where it entrained at 12 midnight. Batt. detrained at 3 p.m. at EDGE HILL Station near DERNANCOURT and proceeded to camp where it stayed for 15th	
	Sept 16th		Batt. moved into billets in DERNANCOURT at 9 a.m. and left billets at 2 p.m. marching to bivouac near FRICOURT	
	Sept 17th Sept 18th		Batt. rested in bivouac. Batt. marched to bivouac in front of BERNAFAY WOOD arriving at 3 a.m.	

WAR DIARY or INTELLIGENCE SUMMARY

Army Form C. 2118.

Place	Date	Hour	Summary of Events and Information	Remarks and references to Appendices
Bivouac near BERNAFAY WOOD.	Sept 19th		Batt. rested in bivouac.	
	Sept 20th		Still in bivouac, rained very heavily all day.	
	Sept 21st		Heavy rain continues. Batt. still in bivouac. Carrying parties for bombs, S.A.A. &c. B. attn supplied.	
	Sept 22nd		Carrying parties for bombs, S.A.A. &c.	
	Sept 23rd		Fine day, spent in cleaning up. Carrying parties supplied as on previous days.	
ASSEMBLY TRENCHES	Sept 24th		Batt. moved up to ASSEMBLY TRENCHES in front of GUEUDECOURT at 6 p.m. Order of march:- 'D' 'C' 'B' 'A' Coys.	
		6 p.m.	The attack was to be carried out in a two platoon frontage, and in eight waves, at 250 yd interval. C & D Coys forming first line - D Coy on left - C Coy on right, with a platoon of each Coy in NEW TRENCH. A Coy in support in GAP TRENCH. - B Coy in reserve in trenches behind GAP TRENCH. Batt. H.Qrs. in LEWIS TRENCH.	
		9 p.m.	Heavy shelling at 9.30 p.m. & 10 p.m. whilst Batt. was getting into position in ASSEMBLY TRENCHES. Lieut Cochrane, R.A.M.C. 2/Lieut Partridge, and 10 O.R. wounded. The night was quiet.	

WAR DIARY
or
INTELLIGENCE SUMMARY.
(Erase heading not required.)

Place	Date	Hour	Summary of Events and Information	Remarks and references to Appendices
	Sept 25th		consolidating and deepening trenches which were very shallow. NEW TRENCH being dug, & foot deep. Batto. reported in position at 2:30 a.m. Patrols from 'C' and 'D' Coys. went out between 1am & 3 a.m. and reported Enemy wire completely arranged and GOAT TRENCH lightly held. The morning was spent in making final preparations for attack. Enemy shelling not heavy and a few casualties were sustained. Scaling traverses formed up in front of trenches.	
		12.35 p.m.	Advance commenced. 'C' and 'D' in extended order – 'A' and 'B' Coys. in Artillery Formation. Enemy immediately commenced an extremely intense and deep barrage.	
		12.37 p.m.	First two platoons of 'B' Coy. reached GIRD TRENCH, but sustained heavy casualties. All Coy. Officers becoming casualties. 2/Lieut. O.E. Pett, 2/Lieut. W.S. Gilbert, C.S.M. Potterton killed, – 2/Lieut. Clark wounded.	
		12.45 p.m.	Remnants of first two waves of 'C' Coy. reached GIRD TRENCH, but owing to M.G. fire from the right and Brigade on the right being	

WAR DIARY
or
INTELLIGENCE SUMMARY.

(Erase heading not required.)

Army Form C. 2118.

Instructions regarding War Diaries and Intelligence Summaries are contained in F.S. Regs., Part II. and the Staff Manual respectively. Title pages will be prepared in manuscript.

Place	Date	Hour	Summary of Events and Information	Remarks and references to Appendices
			Failed to take GIRD TRENCH. The party were all killed or wounded. 2/Lieut Pennie killed in GIRD TRENCH - Lieut Henwood wounded. Capt. Nash collected 3rd and remnant of 'C' Coy and formed a defensive flank down SUNKEN ROAD, facing right.	
		1pm	Capt. Leaf wounded. - C.S.M. Rhodes killed. 'C' Coy suffered extremely heavy casualties from M.G. fire. 'B' Coy advanced and established themselves in NEW TRENCH, BULL TRENCH and PATROL TRENCH. Had been in Batt. Hd. Qrs. advanced from LEWIS TRENCH to PATROL TRENCH. Capt. Allbery led 'A' Coy forward but was severely hit by M.G. fire from the right flank. Lieut. Bready, 2/Lieut Lamb, C.S.M. Rice and many of Coy. becoming casualties. Every man came	
		1.37pm	wounded in arm in PATROL TRENCH. Batt. Hd Qrs. advanced to BULL TRENCH.	
		2.0pm	Remainder of Batt. Hd. Qrs. viz: Lieut. Col. Haig, Capt. Pyhan (& M. Lewis Rogs) Lt. Nash and 3 orderlies advanced to NEW TRENCH. Capt. Pyhan and 3 orderlies wounded.	

WAR DIARY
or
INTELLIGENCE SUMMARY.

(Erase heading not required.)

Army Form C. 2118.

Place	Date	Hour	Summary of Events and Information	Remarks and references to Appendices
		7 p.m.	being either killed or wounded. Heavy shelling all the time. Connection with Brigade established through 2/Lieut. Kelly. During night - R.E.s. constructed a strong point at M.32.A.1.9. Myself and digging in and consolidating position. Enemy seemed to be working round behind PILGRIMS WAY but did not attack.	
	26. Sept.	6 a.m.	From Zero (12.35 p.m.) to 3.30 p.m. Enemy kept up a heavy and very deep barrage, keeping silence at times. A "Tank", supported by bombing party of 7th Leic. Regt. cleared GIRD TRENCH on right of PILGRIMS WAY, taking over 330 prisoners. Patrols from 6th Leic. Regt. and D. & B. Coys. went forward into GEUDECOURT and reported village clear of the Enemy. Remnants of 'C' and 'D' Coys. occupied GIRD TRENCH.	
		8 a.m.	Major Bent reported at Batt. Hd. Qrs. with orders from the General that the Batt. was to be withdrawn to BULL TRENCH and PATROL TRENCH which was carried out at 6 p.m. Intermittent shelling throughout the day, becoming intense about 11 a.m. and 3 p.m.	
	2 p.m.			

WAR DIARY or INTELLIGENCE SUMMARY

Army Form C. 2118.

Place	Date	Hour	Summary of Events and Information	Remarks and references to Appendices
		2.35p	Advance hung up on account of M.G. fire and rifle fire. Enemy still occupying GIRD TRENCH on right of SUNKEN ROAD. Lieut. Col. Haig and Lieut. Toath advanced to NEW TRENCH and finding it empty, crossed over to GOAT TRENCH. Only dead and wounded men were found in GOAT TRENCH. Accordingly Lieut. Col. Haig and Lieut. Toath, in anticipation that the first two Companies had reached GIRD TRENCH, again advanced to PILGRIMS WAY where no O.R. of 8th Leic. Regt. were found without any Officer. Lieut. Col. Haig decided to remain and hold on with no O.R. until reinforcements arrived to clear GIRD TRENCH on right.	
		3.0 p.m.	Connection with 55th Division in GIRD TRENCH on left of PILGRIMS WAY established. Bombing Coys. of 8th and 9th Leic. Regt. were organised and worked down GIRD TRENCH on right of PILGRIMS WAY for 30 or 60 yds. Many of the Enemy killed and 12 taken prisoners. Owing to lack of bombs, a block was established, and a Lewis Gun posted near block. Lieut. Col. Haig sent numerous reports on the situation to Brigade Hd. Qrs., only two of which reached Brigade. He ordered	

Army Form C. 2118.

WAR DIARY
or
INTELLIGENCE SUMMARY.
(Erase heading not required.)

Place	Date	Hour	Summary of Events and Information	Remarks and references to Appendices
		11pm	Batt. had orders to withdraw to SWITCH and GAP TRENCHES which was successfully carried out by 2 a.m. without casualties. Used in consolidating trenches. Batt. found carrying parties from Brigade Hd. Qrs. to GUEUDECOURT nightly. Batt. relieved on the night of 1st-2nd October by 6th Batt. E. Kent Regt. by 1 a.m. & employed at various near BERNAFAY WOOD to Batt. from 2nd Sept. to 1st Oct. - 12 Officers 274 O.R.	
	31.10.16			

P. S. Reed - Major.
Comdg. 7th (Ser.) Batt. The Leicestershire Regt.

"A" Form.
MESSAGES AND SIGNALS.   Army Form C. 2121.

TO: Operation Orders by Lieut. Colonel C. H. Haig.
24-9-16.   No. 12.

AAA

(Ref. 1/10,000 British Front.)

MOVE
The Battn. will relieve part of 15th D.L.I. and take up assembly positions during night of Sept. 24/25th. The Boundary between BLISS & BRACKET will be approximately T.1.d.25.60. — N.31.d.98.65. — N.32.a.33.25.

RELIEF.
The first party will move off from 64th Bde H.Qrs. near YORK Trench (exact position will be notified later) at 6 p.m., remaining parties at 5 minutes interval.
1st party. 2 platoons BLISS followed by 1 platoon D and 1 platoon C of BRACKET will move to NEW TRENCH VIA COCOA LANE — GAS ALLEY moving into trench by WATLING STREET,

"A" Form.
MESSAGES AND SIGNALS.

Army Form C. 2121.

2nd party. 2 platoons BLISS followed by 1 platoon D and 1 platoon C will move by same route into FRONT TRENCH (old front trench with Battery in it.)

3rd party. 2 platoons BLISS followed by 1 platoon D and 1 of C into PATROL TRENCH

4th party. 2 platoons BLISS followed by 1 platoon D and 1 of C into SUPPORT TRENCH

5th party. 2 platoons A Coy followed by 2 platoons BLISS will move via COCOA LANE and FOSSE WAY into LEWIS TRENCH. Guide 2/Lieut Lewis and 2 men A Coy.

2 platoons A Coy followed by 2 platoons BLISS will move via COCOA LANE and FOSSE WAY into GAP TRENCH.

6th party. 2 platoons B Coy followed by 2 platoons BLISS will move via COCOA LANE and FOSSE WAY into Trench in Rear of GAP TRENCH. Guides BLISS.

From: GAP TRENCH
Place:
Time:

"A" Form.
MESSAGES AND SIGNALS.

Army Form C. 2121

7th party. 2 platoons B Coy followed by 2 platoons BLISS will move via same Route into 2nd Trench in Rear of GAP TRENCH
  Guides BLISS.
  Guides will be provided for 1, 2, 3, and 4 parties. BLISS will find guides for 6 & 7 parties.

OTHER UNITS.
  1 section of BOOK M.G Coy will be in FRONT TRENCH and 2 sections in GAP TRENCH.   2 sections of BOOK L.T.M. Battery will be in PATROL TRENCH.

TRENCHES.
  will be improved as much as possible during the hours of darkness but there will be as little movement as possible by day.

"A" Form.
MESSAGES AND SIGNALS.
Army Form C.2121

Artillery Boards which are being issued today will be put up on the parados of all advanced trenches. They must be hidden from enemy.

During the night 24/25th Sept GOAT and GIRD Trenches will be swept at intervals by L.G. Fire to prevent enemy working on his wire.

Completion of relief and arrival in assembly positions will be reported to Bn. H.Qrs. in LEWIS TRENCH by runner.

(Sd) G. Toote 1/Adjt

9th Bn Seventh Regiment

WAR DIARY
or
INTELLIGENCE SUMMARY.

Army Form C. 2118.

Vol #15

Place	Date	Hour	Summary of Events and Information	Remarks and references to Appendices
	Oct 2nd		Battn. moved off from kivia at BERNEFAY WOOD and marched via MONTAUBAN - FRICOURT - MEAULTE to DERNANCOURT where Battn. remained for 3rd October.	
	Oct 3rd		Battn. entrained at EDGE STATION and travelled by train to LONGPRÉ arriving at midnight where it detrained and marched to FRANCIERES.	
	Oct 4-5th		Day spent cleaning up, refitting and re-equipping.	
	Oct 6th			
	Oct 7th		Battn. entrained at PONT-REMY at 9pm and detrained at BETHUNE at 12.30am on the 8th, marching to FOUQUERES-LA-BETHUNE.	
	Oct 8th 9 a.m.		Days spent resting and cleaning up.	
	Oct 9th			
	Oct 10th		Battn. left FOUQUERES and marched to SAILLY-LA-BOURSE where Coys. proceeded by Platoons at 300 yds. interval to the support trenches in the HOHENZOLLERN SECTOR. Battn. was not attached at all. Spent in Support Trenches. Considerable work to be done in these trenches.	
	Oct 11th to 14th			

Army Form C. 2118.

WAR DIARY
or
INTELLIGENCE SUMMARY.
(Erase heading not required.)

Instructions regarding War Diaries and Intelligence Summaries are contained in F.S. Regs., Part II. and the Staff Manual respectively. Title pages will be prepared in manuscript.

Place	Date	Hour	Summary of Events and Information	Remarks and references to Appendices
	Oct 11th to 16th (contd)		Battn. did good work reconstructing and repairing Support Line and Keep.	
	Oct 16th		Battn. relieved the 6th Leic. Regt. in trenches G.4.d.35 to G.5a.9.7. Casualties nil. Enemy Trench Mortars did considerable damage to NORTHAMPTON TRENCH. Our T.M's replied effectively.	
	Oct 17th			
	Oct 18th		Enemy T.M's again active in afternoon to our front. Major P.E. Bent: bounded Battn. aid: dropped 300 yds. handing over right Coy. sector to one Coy. of 8th Leic. Regt. Trenches now held with two Coys. front line and two in RESERVE TRENCH. Sector on the left taken over from 10th K.O.Y.L.I's is in a very bad state, - very little work has been done in these trenches. Trenches now occupied, G.4.d.33 to A.28.c.35v.0.	
	Oct 19th		Day passed quietly.	
	Oct 20th		Patrols went out and reported MAD POINT CRATER to be held by the Enemy, - no Enemy Patrols were encountered.	
	Oct 21st		Battn. was relieved by 6th Battn. Leic. Regt, in the morning. Relief completed without casualties.	

Army Form C. 2118.

WAR DIARY
or
INTELLIGENCE SUMMARY

(Erase heading not required.)

Instructions regarding War Diaries and Intelligence Summaries are contained in F. S. Regs., Part II. and the Staff Manual respectively. Title Pages will be prepared in manuscript.

Place	Date	Hour	Summary of Events and Information	Remarks and references to Appendices
	Oct 28th	6.27 p.m	Battn. moved back into Reserve line in front of VERMELLES. 200 O.R. were supplied to the R.E. for working and carrying parties. No hostile action to report.	
	Oct 29th		Battn. relieved 6th Battn. Leic. Regt. in the front line. relief completed without casualties.	
	Oct 30th		Day passed quietly. the searchlight interfered considerably with our wiring parties. Patrols did useful work. Enemy T.M.'s very active in relation to our T.M. fire. Much greater activity in Rifle Grenades. Patrol went out, but encountered no Enemy.	
	Oct 31st		Wiring parties again interfered with by searchlight. Considerable amount of mine lashes fired out in front of the sector – very little reciprocating Enemy was found. Casualties in Battn. from Oct. 2nd to Oct 31st 1 Officer, 6 O.R.	

31.10.16

P. R. Ryl. Major
Commanding 9th (Ser) Battn. Leicestershire Regt.

9 Kent to Regt
Vol 16

16C
Strats

Army Form C. 2118.

WAR DIARY
or
INTELLIGENCE SUMMARY.
(Erase heading not required.)

Place	Date	Hour	Summary of Events and Information	Remarks and references to Appendices
FRONT TRENCHES, HOHENZOLLERN SECTOR.	Nov. 1st		A mine was blown up on our right about 2 p.m. Batt. "stood to", but no Enemy attack followed, otherwise day passed quietly.	
	Nov. 2nd		Enemy were active with T.M.S and Rifle Grenades, but ceased fire when we retaliated. Enemy "searchlight" again hampered our wiring parties. The Artillery fired a few rounds at it and it disappeared. Our Patrols were out, but did not encounter any Enemy Patrols. The trenches are in a bad state owing to the bad weather, and there are many falls.	
SUPPORT TRENCHES	Nov. 3rd 2 to 4 p.m & 8 p.m		Batt. was relieved by 6th Devon. Regt. – Casualties – nil. Batt. in Support – working parties were found daily for front line. weather very bad and many falls have occurred.	
FRONT TRENCHES	Nov. 9th		Batt. relieved the 6th Batt. Devon Regt. in front trenches – Casualties – nil. Enemy enjoying himself much more than usual. Our Snipers claim several hits.	
	Nov. 10th 8-12 p		Days passed quietly. Our wiring parties and Patrols did good work and were not interfered with by searchlight, which seems to have been knocked out.	

2333 Wt. W2514/1454 700,000 5/15 D.D.&L. A.D.S.S./Forms/C. 2118.

Army Form C. 2118.

WAR DIARY
or
INTELLIGENCE SUMMARY.
(Erase heading not required.)

Instructions regarding War Diaries and Intelligence Summaries are contained in F. S. Regs., Part II. and the Staff Manual respectively. Title pages will be prepared in manuscript.

Place	Date	Hour	Summary of Events and Information	Remarks and references to Appendices
	13th		Enemy rather more active than usual. Large working party was dispersed by our M.G. fire and casualties were inflicted.	
	14th		Nothing to report.	
	15th		Batt. was relieved by 6th Batt. Rev. Regt. Much good work has been done during the tour and all the O.Ts are now open.	
RESERVE TRENCHES.	16th to 20th		Batt. in Reserve - nothing to report. 400 O.R. were furnished daily for R.E.	
FRONT LINE TRENCHES	21st		Batt. relieved the 6th Batt. Rev. Regt. - Casualties nil.	
	22nd		Nothing to report.	
	23rd		Our patrols were active, but none of the Enemy were encountered. T.M.'s slightly more active than usual.	
	24th		At 5.57 A.M. a prisoner belonging to the 165th Regt. 1st Bavn. Res. Div. was taken by our Post in 116. A patrol under 2/Lt. Cox attempted to reach MAD CAP CRATER, but Enemy were held up heavily. Casualties Nil. Enemy made no reply to our bombing.	
	25th to 26th		Enemy extremely active with T.M.'s and considerable damage done to trenches.	

Army Form C. 2118.

WAR DIARY
or
INTELLIGENCE SUMMARY.
(Erase heading not required.)

Place	Date	Hour	Summary of Events and Information	Remarks and references to Appendices
	27th		Battn. was relieved by 6th Battn. Leic. Regt. Casualties NIL.	
	28th & 29th		Battn. in Support Line - working parties furnished for front Battns. The 11th Essex. of 6th Div. took over RAILWAY KEEP & RAILWAY RESERVE	
	30th		TRENCH and B & D Coys. moved back to RESERVE LINE in LANCASHIRE TRENCH.	
			Casualties in Battn. from Nov. 1st to Nov. 30th - 7 O.R.	

P.S. Bunt. Major
Commdg. 9th (Res.) Battn. Leicestershire Regt.

-12-16

Army Form C. 2118.

WAR DIARY
or
INTELLIGENCE SUMMARY.
(Erase heading not required.)

Instructions regarding War Diaries and Intelligence Summaries are contained in F.S. Regs. Part II. and the Staff Manual respectively. Title pages will be prepared in manuscript.

Place	Date	Hour	Summary of Events and Information	Remarks and references to Appendices
Support Trenches	Dec 1-2nd		Battalion in support. Usual working parties found for front line.	
	" 3rd		Battalion relieved 6th Battn. Leicestershire Regt. in the trenches. Casualties NIL.	
Front	" 4th		Enemy T.M's active, little damage done to trenches.	
"	" 5th		Nothing to report.	
	" 6th			
	" 8th		Enemy Artillery slightly more active than usual.	
	" 9th		Battalion relieved by 6th Bn. Leicestershire Regt. Casualties NIL. Battn. moved back into Reserve. 2 Coys. to MAZINGARBE, 2 Coys. and Battn. HQrs. LANCASHIRE TRENCH.	
Reserve	" 10th			
	" 12th		Usual working parties found for R.E.S.	
	" 14th			
	" 15th		Battn. relieved by 15th D.L.I.; 64th Bde. Battn. moved to BETHUNE via SAILLY - LABOURSE - BEUVRY. and went into MONTMORENCY BARRACKS.	
Bethune	" 16-17		Spent cleaning up, refitting etc, musketry drill being carried out in the morning.	
	" 20		Battn. move by Route March via ANNEZIN - CHOQUE'S - PONT DU REVELLON - ALLOUAGNE - LOZINGHEM. - AUCHEL - RAIMBERT. Loon Aillet.	
	" 21-24		Physical Drill, Squad Drill, Musketry & Bayonet fighting carried out daily.	

WAR DIARY
or
INTELLIGENCE SUMMARY.

Army Form C. 2118.

Place	Date	Hour	Summary of Events and Information	Remarks and references to Appendices
RAIMBERT.	25ᵗʰ		Church Parade and celebration of Xmas Day.	
	26-29		Training carried out. Companies carried out short route march.	
	30ᵗʰ		Battalion carried out Route March with transport via FEBFAY BELLERY -AMES - BUBBURE - RAIMBERT.	
	31ˢᵗ		Church Parade. Companies carried out Tactical scheme for Officers & NCO's.	
			Casualties from Dec 1ˢᵗ to 31ˢᵗ - 1. O.R.	

P. Anml Lieut-Colonel
Comdg 9ᵗʰ Leicestershire Regt

WAR DIARY *or* **INTELLIGENCE SUMMARY**
(Erase heading not required.)

Leicester Regt., Army Form C. 2118.

Vol 18

18.C
2 sheets

Place	Date	Hour	Summary of Events and Information	Remarks and references to Appendices
BILLETS RAIMBERT	March 1/Mar 31		Battn. in rest billets at RAIMBERT with Brigade H.Q. and at AUCHEL. During this period. Battn. carried out continuous training daily, consisting mainly of Physical training, Squad Drill, Company Drill, Extended Order Drill, Bayonet fighting etc. A Rifle Range was constructed & the whole Battn. was fired through the majority of the practices in Table A. A Range at LA Bourdinial School, FERFAY was also placed at the disposal of the Battn. on several days during which all "Retained men" fired Part III of Table A. Special classes for Lewis Gunners, Snipers, Signallers, Buglers & Buglers (Cpl) were instituted. Rapid Loading by standing of arm and 2 right arm, was also practised daily. Tactical Talks & Tactical Tours for Officers were also held. Conferences also held stimuli attained for General meeting & Saluting. Batt. Route marched and carried out a few voyages of two per week. A draft of 363 O.R. joined Battn. on the 18th Feb. Instructing drill was given to the draft. The weather on the whole moderately cold turning Brigade Staff	

Army Form C. 2118.

WAR DIARY
or
INTELLIGENCE SUMMARY.
(Erase heading not required.)

Instructions regarding War Diaries and Intelligence Summaries are contained in F.S. Regs., Part II. and the Staff Manual respectively. Title pages will be prepared in manuscript.

Place	Date	Hour	Summary of Events and Information	Remarks and references to Appendices
BILLETS RAMBERT			were held during the period.	
	Jan 26th		The 1st Army Commander Gen. Sir H. HORNE. K.C.B.,	
			The Corps Commander Lieut. Gen. ANDERSON, also the Divisional General, visited the training grounds or armed scheme.	
	Jan 27th		The LOOS SECTOR was visited & reconnoitred by the C.O. & senior officers of the Battn. & preparations made for taking over the part of the line.	
	Jan 28th		All arrangements for taking over LOOS SECTOR cancelled. - Battn. under orders to move at short notice.	
			Battn. marched to LILLERS, where it entrained at 6 P.M. Battn. detrained at PROVEN at 10.30 P.M. & marched to billets in the HOUDEQUE - WATOU Area, arriving in billets at 3 A.M.	
BILLETS	Jan 29th		Battn. in rest. - day spent cleaning up.	
	Jan 30th		C.O. & Company Commanders made a special reconnaissance.	
	Jan 31st		Day spent in training.	
			Casualties for Jan 1st to Jan 31st NIL.	

2.2.17.

P.V.P. Ord Lieut Colonel,
Comdg. 2nd (Ser) Batt. The Leicestershire Regt.

2353 Wt W2544/1454 700,000. 5/15 D. D. & L. A.D.S.S. Forms/C 2118.

9th Lancaster Regt

Army Form C. 2118.

WAR DIARY
or
INTELLIGENCE SUMMARY.
(Erase heading not required).

9th "B" Lincolnshire Regt

Vol 19

19.C
3 whole

Place	Date	Hour	Summary of Events and Information	Remarks and references to Appendices
BILLETS	Feb. 1 & 2nd		Battn. still in HOUTERQUE - WATOU Area	
HOUTERQUE AREA	Feb. 3rd - 6		12 mile via WATOU - PROVEN and along the POPERINGE Rd. Carried out in the afternoon.	
	Feb. 3rd - 6		Battn. carried out usual training, very hard frost prevailed throughout the period.	
	Feb. 10th			
	Feb. 12th		Battn. received orders to entrain at PROVEN Station at 9AM on 13th	
	Feb. 13th		Battn. together with transport, moved by train to BETHUNE.	
	Feb. 14th		Battn. moved into huts at NOEULLES, relieving the 1st Batt. Royal West Kents. - C.O. & Coy Commanders made a reconnaissance of trenches	
TRENCHES HOHENZOLLERN	Feb. 15th		Battn. moved into trenches in the HOHENZOLLERN SECTOR, relieving the 8th Bedfordshire Regt. in the Left. Sub. Sector. - Relief Completed without casualties.	
	Feb. 16th		T.M's fairly active. At 11.45 A.M. fired 6 rockets which burst into double green lights.	
	Feb. 17th		At 10.20 A.M. Enemy heavy artillery fired 12 rounds into VERMEULES	

Army Form C. 2118.

WAR DIARY
or
INTELLIGENCE SUMMARY.
(Erase heading not required.)

Instructions regarding War Diaries and Intelligence Summaries are contained in F. S. Regs. Part II. and the Staff Manual respectively. Title pages will be prepared in manuscript.

Place	Date	Hour	Summary of Events and Information	Remarks and references to Appendices
TRENCHES HOHENZOLLERN			Trench Mortars active. 20 rounds heavy fired from different points, along NORTHAMPTON TRENCH, damage slight. Our light Trench Mortar at junction of NORTHAMPTON TRENCH and SAVILLE ROW registered on Enemy's front line early in the morning.	
	Feb 18th		A few T.M's fell along NORTHAMPTON TRENCH & QUARRY ALLEY during the evening. On the whole the front has been very quiet.	
	Feb 19th		Between 9 A.M. 9.2 P.M. Enemy T.M's NEW CUT & CRATER LINE damaging trench near Post 8. About 30 Rifle Grenades were fired on Posts 8 9 & 10. Enemy did not reply. Considerable movement was noticed this morning opposite Left Sector, indicating a relief. Our Snipers observed the enemy relieving at G.a.a. at 5.0 A.M. The matter was reported to Bde. at 5.20 P.M. & Artillery took action.	
	Feb 20th to 26th		Battn. was in Support, afterwards working parties & garrisoned KEEP LINE.	
	Feb 27th		Battn. relieved 6th Leic. Regt. in front line about 11.0 P.M.	

Army Form C. 2118.

WAR DIARY
or
INTELLIGENCE SUMMARY.
(Erase heading not required.)

Place	Date	Hour	Summary of Events and Information	Remarks and references to Appendices
TRENCHES. HOHENZOLLERN	2/1.28		Day passed quietly. 2 medium 9 light T.M's fell round junction of SAMUEL ROW & NORTHAMPTON TRENCH at 9.30 A.M. At 5.30 P.M. Transport was heard in the vicinity of G.u.t.a.w. which sounded like a Trench Railway. Enemy was seen working just opposite Posts 12 & 13 at 5.45 A.M. Artillery took action & several shells burst amongst them. Total Casualties February 2nd to February 28th 2 O.R. Killed 15 O.R. Wounded (2 died of wounds) Total 17 O.R.	
	2.3.17			

P.S. Rait Lieut Colonel.
Commdg. 2/4(de) Batt. The Leicestershire Regt.

Army Form C. 21

WAR DIARY
or
INTELLIGENCE SUMMARY.

9th Bn. Lincolnshire Regt.

Vol 20

20C
2 sheets

Place	Date	Hour	Summary of Events and Information	Remarks and references to Appendices
TRENCHES Hohenzollern Sector	Mar. 1st		T.M.S. unusually quiet - 4 medium T.M.S. fell at the head of QUARRY ALLEY damaging the trench. Our stokes' retaliated for enemy rifle grenades.	
	Mar. 2nd		At 3:15 am bombardment on our right. Enemy were very excited - large number of very lights were sent up. T.M.S. active during the forenoon - our Field Guns fired intermittently by day & night.	
	Mar. 4th		Our heavys active on back areas.	
	Mar. 5th		Normal activity. Batt. was relieved by 6th Leic. Regt.	
	Mar. 6 to 10th		Usual working parties were found while Batt. was in Reserve.	
	Mar. 11th		Batt. relieved the 6th Leic. Regt. in the trenches	
	Mar. 12/14th		During these days there was very little activity on either side - our Artillery and enemies same	
	Mar. 15th		At 5:0 am. a Brigade Raiding Party, consisting of 150 men, of which we supplied 1 Off. & 40 OR. - raided the enemies trenches. The Raid was successful - we captured one prisoner. it is estimated that 60 casualties were inflicted on the enemy. The Casualties of the Batt.	

WAR DIARY
or
INTELLIGENCE SUMMARY.

(Erase heading not required.)

Army Form C. 2118

Instructions regarding War Diaries and Intelligence Summaries are contained in F. S. Regs., Part II. and the Staff Manual respectively. Title pages will be prepared in manuscript.

Place	Date	Hour	Summary of Events and Information	Remarks and references to Appendices
TRENCHES				
HOHENZOLLERN	Mar 16th		Fairly severe:- 2 O.R. killed & 6 O.R. wounded.	
SECTOR	Mar 17th		Very little activity, no attempts at retaliation for the raid has been made. Relieved by 6th Leic. Regt. in the trenches	
	Mar 22nd to 26th		The Batt. was in the Support line & furnished several working parties. In the evening Batt. moved to the Front line & relieved the 5th Leic Regt.	
	Mar 27th to 28th		No incidents of any importance has happened during the past 4 days. Batt. was relieved in the trenches by 27th Manchester Regt. & proceeded to SPRAY LABOURSE.	
BILLETS SAILLY	Mar 28th		The day was spent in cleaning up, kit inspections etc.	
	Mar 29th		Batt. proceeded by rail to GAUDIEMPRÉ & was billeted there	
BILLETS GAUDIEMPRE	Mar 30th		Cleaning & making available the billets took most of the day.	
	Mar 31st		Batt. carried out Training.	
			Total casualties in Batt. from March 1st to March 31st	9 O.R. killed & died of W. 36 O.R. wounded
			TOTAL	9 O.R. 36 O.R.

P. R. Whyte Lieut Col.
Commdg 9 Ser Batt. Leicester Regt.

Annual references on 6
(S.I.6.S.W) **WAR DIARY** or
(Edn. a/Mirror) **INTELLIGENCE SUMMARY**
(Erase heading not required.)

Army Form C. 2118.

9th Bn. Leinster Regt.

Vol 21

21C
Sheets

Place	Date	Hour	Summary of Events and Information	Remarks and references to Appendices
GOMMECOURT	Oct 25		Battalion carried out usual training	
POMMIER	3rd		Battalion moved by route march to POMMIER (1 Coy BONVILLERS)	
MONCHY-AU-BOIS	4th		Battalion moved by route march to MONCHY-AU-BOIS. Agreeable was found for 1st Battalion [Transport] at the mines of the public and old German dug outs many of which accepted intact	
MOYENNEVILLE	5th		Battalion moved by route march to MOYENNEVILLE via MONCHY-BOYD - BOIRY Bivouacs were constructed from the scrubs and debris of the village	
	6th		Bn in rest at MOYENNEVILLE	
OUTPOST LINE CROISILLES	7th		The Bn relieved the 7. R. Irish Rgt on the outpost line and depicts of CROISILLES + St LEGER. The outpost line [?]. T.S.C. T.17.6. Support T.23.2nd, Reserve T.28.a. (S.I.6.Sd. Ed. 44. 1/40000). The outpost line relieved by daylight. The Lewis Coys holding the outposts in posts to section posts. Enemy completed at 11.30 am. Relief was effected without casualties. Enemy extremely quiet. Patrols went out but found no trace of the enemy	
	8th		Enemy artillery active, but the shelling was not very accurate. Croisilles and old Hindenburg trenches being the chief [?]. An attack was attempted [?] the enemy line in the afternoon. No accurate [?] [?] [?] [?] [?]	

Instructions regarding War Diaries and Intelligence Summaries are contained in F. S. Regs., Part II. and the Staff Manual respectively. Title Pages will be prepared in manuscript.

WAR DIARY
or
INTELLIGENCE SUMMARY
(Erase heading not required.)

Army Form C. 2118.

Place	Date	Hour	Summary of Events and Information	Remarks and references to Appendices
OUTPOST LINE CROISELLES			(Holding Outpost Line T.17.a. – T.17.b.) pushed out a patrol to Cross Rds. T.12.b.3.0. in the early morning & discovered an Enemy Post at T.12.d.6.7. which was estimated to be held by about 30 of the enemy. Our Patrol was unable to reach the Post owing to the moonlight, making it impossible for them to approach without being seen. Right Coy (holding outpost line U.13.c–U.18.b) report that the enemy wire is about 200 yds. from their front line in U.13.b. It is about 6 ft. in height & extremely thick. Our Artillery appears to be firing a little short as the ground in front is pitted with shell holes.	
	April 9th		Our Artillery extremely active on the left, particularly against Enemy line N.34.a. b & d. & T.5.a. At 4.15 P.M. the 64th Bde. on the left attacked HINDENBURG LINE in N.34.a. b & d. & T.5.a. Enemy commenced shelling our Posts & the whole area of the outpost line very heavily. The village of CROISELLES was also heavily shelled with 5.9's & 4.2's. About 5 P.M. 2 Enemy Aeroplanes flying high commenced rapid fire with a Machine Gun, our men in Post in T.18.b, thinking there was a fight going on looked up. One of the Enemy Aeroplanes immediately dived low over the Post & dropped a red light – this Post was very heavily shelled 5 minutes afterwards. About 7 P.M. report was received that the 64th Bde. had taken the Front Line & part of the Support Line of the CO[illegible] SWITCH in the squares N.34. b & d & T.5.a. Our Patrols were again active – Patrols from the Right Coy reached the HINDENBURG Wire & confirmed reports on previous day. Patrol from the Left Coy. made a reconnaissance of the Enemy Posts in T.12.d.6.7. & report that the Sunken Rd. from U.7.c.3.5.–4.0. to T.12.b.2.0. is held by the Enemy with forward Posts at T.12.d.6.7. & T.12.d.[illegible] No further news yet received of the attack on the left. During the Afternoon we suffered 6 casualties & one Lewis Gun was destroyed in the Post in T.18.b.6.3.	
	April 10th		Situation on the left is still very obscure. Usual shelling of the outpost line & CROISELLES during the day with increased activity towards dusk. About 6 P.M. report was received that the Enemy counter attacked the 64th after a short, intense bombardment & had driven them from the trenches in the HINDENBURG LINE & 64th Bde are reported to be holding Posts in front of the wire. Offensive Patrols were out all night. Patrol from the Right Coy. encountered a Patrol of the Enemy close to the HINDENBURG wire in U.13.b.1.6. – our Patrol attacked the Enemy Patrol, which ran back through a gap in the wire close to this spot. Capt Morley killed & 2nd Lieut Parker M.C. wounded in CROISELLES.	
	April 11th		Artillery on both sides very active. Sunken Rds in T.18.c & T.17.d heavily shelled. During the Afternoon situation became quieter. At 8.15 P.M. 'C' Coy in Support relieved 'A' Coy in the Right Outpost Sector.	

2449 Wt. W14957/M90 750,000 1/16 J.B.C. & A. Forms/C.2118/12.

Army Form C. 2118.

WAR DIARY
or
INTELLIGENCE SUMMARY
(Erase heading not required.)

Instructions regarding War Diaries and Intelligence Summaries are contained in F. S. Regs., Part II. and the Staff Manual respectively. Title Pages will be prepared in manuscript.

Place	Date	Hour	Summary of Events and Information	Remarks and references to Appendices
OUT POST LINE CROISELLES	April 29		"A" Coy withdrawing to Support. B. 12. nothing to report. D. Coy returned 2 Platoons to B. Bn. in the Pocket line of the Reft. Bn. 2 Platoons of D. Bn. withdrawn to this Reserve. Patrols were sent to report that the enemy was withdrawing from the HINDENBURG LINE at the eight Supply line. Patrols worked independently pushed forward & penetrated the following points L7.2.35.40 - L7.0.15.6 - T.12.6.3.0 Patrols were able to tell it. Our Polls that were in T.12.A. line from T.12.A. For a time they were the hill of our Polls, that were in T.12.A. Report from Left Coy reached Bn. HINDENBURG LINE in T.12.A. that one Platoon from right Coy had been forced to return owing to M.G. fire. Our Patrols regained in T.12.A. our own M.G. fire. HINDENBURG LINE & Patrol Line 9. was slightly wounded.	
	April 24		CROISELLES again heavily shelled. An attack on our left was made against the Enemy position in the N.W. of CROISELLES. The attack was followed immediately by hostile shelling of our Patrol Posts, but failed of any aim of our line in the days. It was noticed early on through the Enemy wire 7.3.A. but after Battle of a energetic nature it was withdrawn. Many of the Enemy were observed moving in T.12.2.8.9.21 shelling appeared to deal effectively with them. Polls beyond were shelled by M.G.'s which Pets 7.12.1.7.3.	
	April 26		Polls carefully posted in the evening, the 2nd Grenadier Regt. 33rd Brigade relieved Belly Brigade at 2:30 AM at 9 P.M. the snow shelled shelter KLT. T.18.0.97.14A very heavily with 5"9. 9+8. causing several casualties. Belt. withdrew to trenches in HAMELINCOURT starting the could situation weather conditions were extremely bad, & the men suffered from exposure to the open ground.	
BAILLEUL	April 26/27 night		Batt. arrived at HAMELINCOURT - about 2:30 AM arrived in by road.	
AYETTE	April 27 (to AYETTE) April 22nd		Batt. carried out training of all Grenades.	
	April 23rd		Company Parade. to the 20th the Batt. Observed Armed Weapons practices with Line Guns.	
HAMELINCOURT	April 25th		Batt. moved by Route March to HAMELINCOURT via NOYENNEVILLE.	
	April 21st		Batt. in rest at AYETTE. Batt. moved by Route March to HAMELINCOURT. Batt. on road between HAMELINCOURT & AYETTE when it bivouacked for the night.	

WAR DIARY
or
INTELLIGENCE SUMMARY

Army Form C. 2118.

(Erase heading not required.)

Place	Date	Hour	Summary of Events and Information	Remarks and references to Appendices
	April 27th		Orders received that Bath. is to attack the HINDENBURG LINE from SUNKEN ROAD, T.6.d. to S. ROAD U7.b.20.- U.7.b.4.4. Two Tanks to assist in conjunction with the attack - meeting the HINDENBURG Support Coy. C. along the HINDENBURG Road North West to front a support line. T.6.d. assisted in a South Easterly direction from fifty yards N.W. of the SUNKEN ROAD T.6.d. but Brigade told the HINDENBURG LINE N.W. of the SUNKEN ROAD T.6.d. all preparations made for the attack & following regiments formed up. The attack to extend to take about 9 following zero. 1.30 P.M. orders received that the attack is cancelled.	
BOIRY BECQUERELLE	April 29th April 30th		Bath. moved by Route March to BOIRY BECQUERELLE carried on training under Coy. arrangements. Total casualties from April 1st to 6 April 30th. Lieut. J.W. Martin Killed 2/Lieut. C.R. Sayard Killed Lieut. O.D.P. Peake Wounded 9 O.R. Killed 39 O.R. Wounded 6 O.R. Missing 9	

30.4.17

[signature] Lieut Col

Commdg 2/4th Bath. The Leicestershire Regt.

9th Bn Loya Army Form C. 2118.
9th B. [Leinster?] R

Vol 22

22C
9 sheets

WAR DIARY
INTELLIGENCE SUMMARY

Place	Date	Hour	Summary of Events and Information	Remarks and references to Appendices
BOIRY-BECQUERELLE	1st May		At 7 pm the Bn left BOIRY-BECQUEREUE and moved up into forward area. May took our tracks from one Coy of 6th N. Lancs in BROWN LINE from O.31.C.3.6.6. O.31.C.80.10. (Ref Map 57.B.S.G 2 ed 4 Hours), Bay in trenches Rd O.31.C. N.36.6, & Sq in front N.36.6 N.M Trench Rd O.36.9 in front point N.30.C.	
	2nd May		Day spent in completing arrangements for attack on FONTAINE-LES-CROISILLES Bay forming up in advance of BROWN LINE, & Alo in BROWN LINE ode of Battle	
			D Q in rear of A & Cq in rear of D Cq Battalion in position	
	3rd May	3.15am 3.45am	Battalion moved forward to attack. Heavy enemy barrage opened immediately in front of BROWN 2.1415. M.C. fire opened strong from right & left flank, and from O.2.0.2.6. Heavy casualties were suffered from enemy barrage. CAPT. F.A. COX killed. Whilst around	
		4 am	The attacking troops on left flank of Bn came across Bn front pushing our troops to the right. A Tank advanced down WOOD TRENCH but was forced to return owing to M.G. fire 2/Lt Munro 2/Lt Coppock 2/Lts HERSAY 2/Lt WRIGHT wounded	
		4.15am	attack held up in front of FONTAINE trench (Tunnel trench U.16.4.2.a.)	

WAR DIARY
or
INTELLIGENCE SUMMARY

(Erase heading not required.)

Army Form C. 2118.

Place	Date	Hour	Summary of Events and Information	Remarks and references to Appendices
	3rd	5 am	Situation obscure. Runners sent forward with message of 6 aye [?] but none returned	
		7 am	Stoller outpost with S.O.S. and L.G. fired down WOOD TRENCH (see attached map). 2nd Lieut. Telford & Unidaye wounded.	
		7 am	Report received from Stoller. 152 enemy were holding Rumilly R⁰ in front of FONTAINE 600D M[achine] [Gun] in position, Om was holding a line of shell holes along road in front of road. Telephone communication established in WOOD TRENCH but could not of 3rd Army & much valuable information	
		8.45 am	Message received from Capt. Milburne 2nd Lieut. was holding a brick wall. 1 Officer & 30 O.R. with enemy on both flanks and in front. He was unable to advance his frontier and [?] any further to retire back.	
		11.40 am	Report received from Liaison officer with Battalion on our left. 2nd Bn on left had withdrawn. Communication with 2nd Bn extremely difficult wires being continually cut	
		12 noon	Report received from Bde HQrs that the attack of the 6th SWB on the right in the HINDENBURG LINE had made no progress.	

WAR DIARY
or
INTELLIGENCE SUMMARY

Army Form C. 2118

Place	Date	Hour	Summary of Events and Information	Remarks and references to Appendices
	3rd May	4.30	Continued machine gun and rifle fire and communication by runner in forced rifle. Message received from Lt. Scott (or May) in reserve 00. He stated this runner had been a long distance trying to get help as he had to move from shell hole to shell hole every few minutes to avoid fire. Message stated 1500 West coast area at 02.a.6 with 2 other officers + 200 R. Enemy was around bombing down PONTAINE Trench and had commenced working around the flanks of the party	
		7.30	Enemy opened a heavy bombardment of BRGANINES and appeared to consolidate F.6.7.8.8 Leasely Rifle Trenches near to consolidate - attacking. All troops in BROWN LINE and Leasely Rifle Trenches near here beautiful bombarded although the enemy taken carrying parties were seen coming up and "plated 6" in Support trench north in rear of BROWN LINE	
		8.30	Enemy barrage still continued on BROWN LINE. L.G. hooks were pushed forward from BROWN LINE	
		9.30	Enemy barrage slackened considerably and ceased shortly. 13th Northumberland Fusiliers would take our 10 minute Orders received 15th 13th Northumberland Fusiliers would take our 10 minute Orders received 15 Btn by 6 Brigade and that all advance posts of Maison 110" BROWN LINE held by the 6 Brigade and that all advance posts of Trench Left Btt were to be withdrawn	
	4th May	2 am	Remnants of Battalion withdrew to Helples on M. 36.c.05.30 & M. 36.c.30.60. and reorganised. Total casualties from May 2nd to May 4th: 16 officers 299 OR	

WAR DIARY
or
INTELLIGENCE SUMMARY
(Erase heading not required.)

Army Form C. 2118.

Place	Date	Hour	Summary of Events and Information	Remarks and references to Appendices
	May 1st May 6 to 8		Battn. northern to Bivouac in the QUARRY ST LEGER. Battn. in Reserve in the QUARRY ST LEGER.	
	May 9		Cleared up. Battn. relieved by 16th K.R.R.B. and Bde. marched back to billets in POMMIER via MOYENNEVILLE - AYETTE - DOUCHY LES AYETTE - MONCHY - BIENVILLERS arrived in billets 11.30 P.M.	
	May 10 to May 31st		Battn. in Rest at POMMIER. Training carried out daily. A Range was established at HANNES CAMP & all ranks put through about musketry course. Tactical Exercises for Officers & N.C.O.s & musketry for N.C.O.s were carried out	

Total Casualties from May 1st to May 31st :

2 Officers killed.
10 " Wounded (one severe) 38 O.R. killed
4 " missing   179 O.R. wounded
--   92 O.R. missing
16 Officers   ---
                      301 O.Ranks

O.S Pearl
Lieut Col.
Commdg 2nd Battn. The Leicestershire Regt.

June 3rd 1917

WAR DIARY
or INTELLIGENCE SUMMARY

Situation obscure. Runners & C. Forward with messages by led were returned. I ordered sections with 5 O.R. and L.G. to work down WOOD TRENCH (one alternate way) to that even it were wounded that several Halftracks + enemy M.G. were shooting R.H. + L.H. of FORTUNE WOOD + TRIAGE in strength. Our men holding tour out flank and slimmer remained in WOOD FRENCH until night of 5th sending much valuable information.

Major Millner was now holding a broken line of war + 300 R and enemy in the flanks up in the are made no attempt to penetrate and Coates set no troops on their flank. As not received from known offices with battalion on our left that bath on in R had undertaken communication with his his extremely difficult.

Runner received from Enemy at 10.15 in attack of the 61st Made on its right on the Hohenzollern Rove had made no progress.

WAR DIARY
or
INTELLIGENCE SUMMARY

Army Form C. 2118

Place	Date	Hour	Summary of Events and Information	Remarks references to Appendices
	5th June		Continued Machine gun fire and during night communications by runner unavoidable.	
		5:30	Barrage resumed from 5 T 30 E (90°N 0y) in answer to enemy's own. It had been of use getting to B Hdqrs as to men to tell relieving enemy for message stated Hy A/Coll was at U.2.a.1.6 and it had gone to OR. Enemy was resumed bombing down FONTAINE trench and had commenced working round the flanks of this party.	
			Enemy turned a heavy bombardment of BROWN LINE and started attacking all troops in BROWN LINE and were compelled to quickly attack the enemy when carrying parties were brought up and and 6" and mortar crews ROYAL WEST BROWN	
		6:15	LIVE	
		6:30	The enemy barrage did continued on BROWN LINE. L. G. toads were marked. Figure was RROWN LINE Enemy barrage weakness Considerably and eased about 9.15 hr Message order received to Northumberland Fusiliers would take over the BROWN LINE relief by the Brigade and that all relieved parts of 11th & 12th Btn were to be withdrawn	
		H.00 am	A march of Battalion address Brunton at N.36.6.65.30. B not to do so and weapons that Casualties arm Nay 2nd & Majors R.Offices & 239 OR	

WAR DIARY or INTELLIGENCE SUMMARY

Army Form C. 2118

(Ref. Instr. 51. & S.W. Hagro & Gen. Intelligence Map.)

9th Leicester Regt Vol 2

23.C.
6 sheets

Place	Date	Hour	Summary of Events and Information	Remarks and references to Appendices
POMMIER	June 1st		Batt. moved by route march to "B" Camp MOYENNEVILLE via BIENVILLERS - BERLES-AU-BOIS - DOUCHY-LES- AYETTE.	
MOYENNEVILLE	June 2nd to 6th		Batt. in Reserve in "B" Camp, MOYENNEVILLE. During the period the Coy was constructed & permanent lines formed. Winter rifles, automatic Coehorns etc. tested.	
TRENCHES	June 7th		Batt. relieved the 10/13 Leicesters Regt. & 12/nd Bde. in the right sub-sector of the Divisional Front trenches from U/13. c.2.1 to U/7.d.2.2. in BURG LANE. Batt. Hd. Qrs. at Coy 19.9.1.2. Batt. left Camp /by Platoons at 2 mins interval/ at 7.30 p.m. Relief complete at midnight without casualties.	
	June 8th		Day passed quietly. Enemy T.M's active in vicinity of NELLY AVENUE. Patrols were out all night but reported no enemy. Wire German wire at U/13.c.9.5. was investigated & found to be uncut though not old. Weather a considerable distance.	
	June 9th		Enemy shelled Batt. area heavily with 5.9's & 4.2's. Rl.11.30pm. Enemy T.M's continually active. A heavy T.M is entering BURG TRENCH from U.M. 0.20 p.m. N.C.O's were also active during the night. The enemy appears to be using the contour near the ridge & was quite quiet during the sight & did little harm in front of our wire obstacle.	Much wire
	June 11th		Batt. H.Q. moved to the Quarry at U/3.c.0.7. Batt was relieved by the 7th Bn. Leicestershire Regt. (110th Bde) during the morning & moved to GUARDIAN TRENCH (3 Coys.) to support Trench & out in Nomad's of Way /QUARRY/. Total interchange except that the 6 + 9 T.M. Bn Bde would attack TUNNEL TRENCH (n. the 13th inst.) - 9th Bn. being in support. Casualties were subsequently reserved that the attack was postponed for at least one hour.	
	June 12th		C Coy in GUARDIAN TRENCH & moved & out played supporting or flanks of offensive by 300 O.R. offlied for carrying - working in Tunnels in the QUARRY etc. by night.	GUARDIAN TRENCH was shelled.
	June 13th		Considerable amount of work done in NELLY AVENUE. Deepening & widening, 30 O.R. outfited for carrying work in QUARRIES. GUARDIAN TRENCH was again shelled during the night.	Parties
	June 14th		Enemy first and very apparently intended that attack anticipated for on the morning. The 35th Division would attack the BURG TRENCH from the HUMP northwards to R.J.M. on the morning of the 15th June. At 9.13 a.m. Cumberland & HELLES (in conjunction with the 33 F. Cameron on right) forced TUNNEL TRENCH from 2 Company to U/11a.6.4. 8 K.R. Leic. Regt. on the left & 9 N.F. Rec Regt. on the right were to be afflicted to 13 & 9.12. N.58. rapidly were reduced to occupy BURG & MOEIN TRENCH & Z'ZAG. BOUNDARY between Batt. & Lord CURRANT LANE. On the failure of the N.C.B, the R. Rt. of 9 N Bn. Leic. Regt.	

Army Form C. 2118

WAR DIARY
or
INTELLIGENCE SUMMARY
(Erase heading not required.)

Instructions regarding War Diaries and Intelligence Summaries are contained in F.S. Regs., Part II. and the Staff Manual respectively. Title Pages will be prepared in manuscript.

Place	Date	Hour	Summary of Events and Information	Remarks and references to Appendices
	June 10th		were to try & prevent Bosche lying any the attack, at short notice. the attack was ordered to form forward dumps for the 13 & 13/134 N.F.S. in BURG TRENCH & to carry up the following material: Relieve 5.10 A.M. 9.12 mm. in the 15th unit. 80 boxes S.A.A. 10,000 Mills Grenades. 2,000 Rifle Grenades. 1000 very lights 200 P.bombs. 100 felix bombs. 2000 sandbags. 1000 shovels, 40 picks, 32 filled Rum jars, 2 R.E.Bund, 40 gals of water. Carrying up to commence before start of attack. 2500 for the attack. The 5.10 P.M. attack is not to be started at 9.50 A.M. Particulars received that the 2&1/8th N.F.S. would carry up to attack on TUNNEL TRENCH & would relieve the 8 & 9 F. One Rif. Regt. in the night of 9/10th. Arrangements for putting down concealed dumps afterwards made by 9 & 6 P. Rif. Regts. formed for night of 15/16th. Bn. Front was carrying parties for the 9 DURRY Party for 10 & 10 P.S. Coys. 200 O.R. were employed in digging the Demolition trenches as at the head of FACTORY AVENUE & in NELLY AVENUE to join with BURG TRENCH. 60 O.R. were employed extending & deepening the head of NELLY AVENUE. Parties commenced work at 10.0 p.m. & finished at 2.25 A.M. having dug two G inch trenches 75 yds long forming a Y at the heads of the two communication trenches NELLY & FACTORY AVENUES.	
	June 10th		Attack of 5th Bn. commenced at 2.50 A.M. TRENCH for 3 1/4 hour at 10.0 A.M. The enemy put down a heavy barrage on GUARDIAN shells. a high velocity naval gun also fired with great accuracy on GUARDIAN TRENCH. the Colo. Dumpt at O.13.0.1.6. 9 the QUARRY the Bosche had approximately 40 Casualties during the morning & many men wounded. As the working strength of the Battn. was now about 350 O.R. the men who had been digging until 2.30 A.M. were ordered to half work the carrying of material from Bde. Dumps to forward Dumps. all available men worked from 5.0 p.m. Carrying up & all dumps were complete by 9.30 p.m. The Bn. of 9 batt. O.T.s were posted Circumstances & the carrying parties which had to fall through the shelling & and journey. Last night the carrying parties returned to GUARDIAN TRENCH at 10.30 p.m. & Casualties attached until 11.15 p.m. 2 Lt E. A. Coffel wounded. at 2.30 A.M. Coys. commenced moving up O.T.s. A & C Coys moved up FACTORY AVENUE, B & D Coys up NELLY AVENUE. Coys were to occupy BURG TRENCH. A & D Coys. LINCOLN TRENCH	

Army Form C. 2118

WAR DIARY
or
INTELLIGENCE SUMMARY

(Erase heading not required.)

Instructions regarding War Diaries and Intelligence Summaries are contained in F.S. Regs., Part II. and the Staff Manual respectively. Title Pages will be prepared in manuscript.

Place	Date	Hour	Summary of Events and Information	Remarks and references to Appendices
	June 16th	at ZERO 3.10 A.m.	During the relief of the 6th & 7th Bat. Leic. Regt. by the 13th & 12th N.F.S. the enemy shelled the back area continuously. At 12.G.O.m. commenced shelling GUARDIAN TRENCH, LONDON TRENCHES & N.F.3 through the barrage at 3.10 a.m.	
		12.0 a.m.	Reports from wounded state that the attack on the left was held up by heavy wire, but that the right had gone forward.	
		6.0 m.	Report from two wounded men confirm that the attack had been held up.	
		12 noon.	Bath. received orders to be prepared to attack that evening, all arrangements were made accordingly.	
		9.0 p.m.	Instructions received that the 6 & 7 Lt. Regt Batts. might be ordered to carry out an attack at short notice.	
	June 17.		Orders received to carry on with wiring the front line & consolidation of pot 9. & gaps of trenches which had been made good by the attacking troops. During the night the 12 & 13 N.F.5 were relieved & reorganised & were as follows: A & D Coys. in BURG TRENCH. C Coy. in night. A & D Coys. in BURG TRENCH. B Coy. in LINCOLN TRENCH, CURRANT LANE & BURG TRENCH from O.13. to 9 X/17. & position CURRANT LANE & heavily shelled causing casualties. During night 16/17. & 17/18. LINCOLN TRENCH would carry out an attack on TUNNEL TRENCH & 6 & 12. Leic. Regt. Instructions were received that the 6 & 7 Lt Lec Regt would push forward along points to U.7. d 6.5 (approx.) & take & hold TUNNEL TRENCH at ZERO. Orders for attack was subsequently cancelled. Balts had ordered to resume work on same lines. Strong patrols were pushed forward to keep in	
			touch with N.5.3.	
	June 18th		During the night, the enemy destroyed LINCOLN TRENCH in many parts, causing heavy casualties to B. Coy. D. Coy were ordered to consolidate LINCOLN TRENCH between A & C Coys. The strength of B. Coy. was new 35. O.R.	
	June 19th		Bay. fell in north of the Boug. Road. Bath. relieved by the 2nd Bn. Royal Irish Fusiliers	
	June 20th		& Camp NOVENNEVILLE, arriving in Camp at 3.0 a.m.	

1875 Wt. W 593/826 1,000,000 4/15 J.B.C. & A. A.D.S.S./Forms/C. 9118.

WAR DIARY or INTELLIGENCE SUMMARY

Army Form C. 2118.

Place	Date	Hour	Summary of Events and Information	Remarks and references to Appendices
	June 28	16.30	Bath. march to BLAIRVILLE via BOIRY ST. RICTRUDE, - HENDECOURT. arriving in Hillside at 6.30 P.M. Bath. at rest. First two days spent reorganising & clearing up. During this period Bath. carried out training & had individual parades in to Platoon & Company in attack. Bn. had 2 eh. Bath. carried out field firing. Total Casualties in Bath. from June 1st to June 30th. 2 officers killed, other ranks 18 killed. 2 officers wounded. 89 wounded, 1 missing. Total. 2 officers. 108 other ranks.	
30.6.17				

P S Burnett Lieut. Col.
Comm. d'g. 9th (Sv.) Bn. The Leicestershire Regt.

WAR DIARY or INTELLIGENCE SUMMARY

Army Form C. 2118.

9th Bn Leicester Regt
57 & S.W. 1/20000. Sh 4.

Vol 24

24 C
2 sheets

Place	Date	Hour	Summary of Events and Information	Remarks and references to Appendices
	7th July		Battalion in Rest at "B" Camp MONZNNEVILLE, during this time a Special Course of Bayonet fighting was carried out under the direction of the Brigade Bayonet Instructor.	
	8th July		The Battalion relieved the 1st East Yorkshire Regt. in Reserve to the right Brigade Sector. T22 a & c. Relief complete without casualties.	
	9th to 13th July		Battalion in Reserve. Working Parties at 4.00 A.M. found daily.	
	14th July		Battalion relieved 7th Battalion Leic. Regt. in the right Brigade Sector. (U.13.c.9.0 to U.7.d.4.1)	
	15th July		The day passed without incident. Enemy Light Trench Mortars fired during the morning, but all shots fell short of our trench. Patrols were out all night, but encountered no enemy Patrols.	
	16th July		Enemy very quiet, during the night the bombs his own Wire, about 6. A.M. an Enemy Aeroplane flew over. Enemy fired White & Green Lights 11-50 P.M. a Yellow coloured flare was observed near HENDECOURT this was followed by a burst of Enemy Artillery fire on our Support. No enemy Patrols encountered.	
	17th July		Nothing to report.	
	18th July		At 11-15 A.M. Enemy shelled the Quarry at T18. V.8.3. with shells of very heavy calibre. One Hund Shell penetrated a dug-out in the Quarry leaving a hole 19 inches in diameter.	
	19th July		Nothing to report.	
	20th July		Battalion moved into Support on relief by 7th Bn. Leic. Regt. on the 21st and remained in Support until 25th. Numerous working parties were found daily for Front line and R.E. work.	
	21st July 16.25.			

2449 Wt. W14957/M90 750,000 1/16 J.B.C. & A. Forms/C.2118/12.

WAR DIARY
or
INTELLIGENCE SUMMARY

Army Form C. 2118.

Place	Date	Hour	Summary of Events and Information	Remarks and references to Appendices
	26 July		Battalion relieved the 7th Battn. Leic. Regt. on the right Tunnel Sector (U.m.a.a.t.5.U.p.d.+.0) during the morning. Bronelles N12.	
	27th		Nothing to report. Our Patrols met with no opposition.	
	28.29th 8.30 8.31st		Enemy unusually inactive. On the nights of the 29th & 30th two Companys Mount rifled fire on Tunnel Trench and the Enemy replied by shelling Battn. H.Q. Qrs. and the Battalions on our right and left. Total casualties for period July 1st to July 31st:- 2 Officers wounded. 2 O. Ranks Killed. 14 O. Ranks wounded.	

2.8.17

Commdg. 9th Bn. the Leicesters Regt.

Army Form C. 2118

9th Leicester Regt.

Vol 25

25C
1 sheet

WAR DIARY
or
INTELLIGENCE SUMMARY
(Erase heading not required.)

Place	Date	Hour	Summary of Events and Information	Remarks and references to Appendices
Aug 1st				
MOYENNEVILLE	Aug 3rd to Aug 8th		Battalion was relieved in the Trenches by the 10th E. Yorks Regt and moved back into Divisional Reserve at "B" Camp MOYENNEVILLE. Relief complete without casualties. Battalion at MOYENNEVILLE. Time spent in training. Tactical Exercises for Officers. One Coy. sent on detachment to ST LEGER for work on Trenches under C.R.E. Organised sports every afternoon.	
CROISILLES TRENCHES	Aug 9th		Battalion relieved 10th E. Yorks. Regt in Brigade Reserve.	Working parties of 360 o.r. found.
"	Aug 9th to Aug 14th		Battalion in Brigade Reserve. Working parties of 350 o.r. found daily, chiefly on work under R.E. supervision. Course of Instruction in repair of Trenches for Officers under 95 Field Coy R.E. Battalion was shelled lightly during the night of 14th & 15th with Gas shells.	
	Aug 14		Battalion was relieved by the 5th/Lth the Queens Regt., and moved back into Divisional Reserve at ERVILLERS. One Coy sent on detachment to ST LEGER to be used for work on Communication Trenches under the orders of the C.R.E.	
ERVILLERS	Aug 18th to Aug 24th		Battalion in Divisional Reserve at ERVILLERS. Training carried on from 8.30 am to 12.30 pm daily. Special instruction in Physical Training and Bayonet fighting by an Instructor from Third Army. Officers Riding Classes in the evening of Brig Batt P22ad. Sports, wiring competitions etc every afternoon.	
GUOY EN ARTOIS	Aug 25th		Battalion moved by motor bus to GUOY EN ARTOIS.	
IZEL LEZ HAMEAU	Aug 26th		Battalion marched to IZEL LEZ HAMEAU.	
IZEL LEZ HAMEAU	Aug 27th to Aug 31st		Battalion in rest at IZEL LEZ HAMEAU. Training from 8.30 am to 12.30 pm. Tactical Exercises for Officers. Organised Sports for afternoons. One or two Coys per day firing field Practices on RANGE. Classes for N.C.O.s	
			Total Casualties period Aug 1st to Aug 31st 1917. - 1 O.R. Wounded.	

1.9.17

1875 Wt. W593/826 1,600,000 4/15 J.B.C. & A. A.D.S.S./Forms/C. 2118.

W Ryle Lt Colonel
Commdg. 9 (Res) Bn. The Leicestershire Regt.

Army Form C. 2118.

WAR DIARY
or
INTELLIGENCE SUMMARY.
(Erase heading not required.)

9th Bn Lincolnshire Regt

Vol 2

26.C
2 sheets

Place	Date	Hour	Summary of Events and Information	Remarks and references to Appendices
IZEL LEZ HAMEAU	Sept 1/2 to 4th		Battalion in Billets at IZEL LEZ HAMEAU. Training carried out daily. N.C.O.s attended a special 6 days course of Physical Training and Bayonet fighting at MANIN. Organised 4000 yds very afternoon. Tactical Exercises and Company marching for Officers were carried out during the evenings. On the night of Sept 21st/22nd, Battalion moved by Route March to SAVY, where it entrained and proceeded to CAESTRE.	
CAESTRE.	Sept 22nd Sept 23rd		Battalion in Camp at CAESTRE. Training carried out daily. Tactical Exercises for Officers and senior N.C.O.s	
METEREN.	Sept 23rd Sept 24th Sept 25th		Battalion moved by Route March to BERTHEN AREA. Kept CAESTRE at 7-30 a.m. more complete by 10-30 am. Battalion in very scattered billets in BERTHEN AREA. Training carried out under Company arrangements. All Officers and senior N.C.Os attended a lecture, given by the Brigade Commander on Defensive.	
LA CLYTTE HALLEBAST.	Sept 26 Sept 26th 28th		Battalion moved to MICMAC Camp of this more complete by 12-30 p.m. Brigade in Corps Reserve. Two hours training carried out daily by Battalion under Coy. arrangements.	

T2134. Wt. W708—776. 500000. 4/15. Sir J. C. & S.

Place	Date	Hour	Summary of Events and Information	Remarks and references to Appendices
	Sep 29		Battalion moved to camp West of Battalion mover in Forward Area at 4.25 c.5.5. by route march. Move complete by 11.30 a.m. Some hostile aeroplane activity at night. One O.R. slightly wounded.	
	Sep 30		Battalion relieved the 32nd Australian Inf Battalion in shell holes E. of POLYGON WOOD in J.11.c. Relief complete before midnight - Casualties Nil.	
			Total Casualties for period from Sept 1st to Sept 30th. Killed — Nil Wounded — 1 O.R.	
			A. Willett Lieut & Adjt. for Lt. Col. comndg 1/4th (Ter.) Bn The Leicestershire Regt.	

Army Form C. 2118.

WAR DIARY
or
INTELLIGENCE SUMMARY.
(Erase heading not required.)

9th Leicester Regt.

Vol 27

27.C.
7 sheets

Place	Date	Hour	Summary of Events and Information	Remarks and references to Appendices
Trenches in	1917			
	1st	4-0 A.M.	Situation reported Normal by Companies.	
front of POLYGON Wood.		5.25 A.M.	Enemy put down heavy barrage on front Company and POLYGON Wood and at the same time put up a smoke screen all along Battalion Front.	
J.16.a.4.9.6.		5.27 A.M.	Enemy attacked though smoke screen. C.O.'s sent the first wave of enemy down off by "A" Coy by Lewis Gun & Rifle fire. Capt A.Q.D. Lee M.C killed.	
J.10.8.7.3.				
		5.30 A.M.	Enemy second wave driven off on our front but enemy attacked on Battalion of Right flank of "A" Coy (front line Coy) sustained. Right flank successful.	
		5.40 A.M.	2 Platoons of B.Coy (who were in Reserve from J.10.2.1.3 to J.10.2.1.1.) and the Lewis Guns of Q.E. Rent. D.L.O. and B.Coy (who were in Support from J.10.c.6.4 & J.10.c.6.0) under Lieut Burn immediately counter-attacked enemy. Bomb attack was entirely successful and there enemy from our front. Lieut Col Burn Killed whilst leading the charge.	
		5.45 A.M.	Enemy continued to make hostile on right flank in J.16.a. and launched his 3rd Wave against our front. This Platoon "B" Coy did not to counter-attack enemy on our right flank. Lieut Burn Killed.	
		6.0 A.M.	"B" Coy Lewis gun attack reported to have stopped enemy attack. 2 Platoons "G" Coy sent up to reinforce and to get in touch with troops on right flank who had been	

WAR DIARY
or
INTELLIGENCE SUMMARY.
(Erase heading not required.)

Army Form C. 2118.

Instructions regarding War Diaries and Intelligence Summaries are contained in F. S. Regs., Part II. and the Staff Manual respectively. Title pages will be prepared in manuscript.

Place	Date	Hour	Summary of Events and Information	Remarks and references to Appendices
	Oct 9th		driven back some distance. Enemy attacking kept driven off but owing to heavy casualties in front Bay, a defensive line was organised approximately 100 yards in rear of our front line, along S. edge of POLYGON WOOD. Enemy shelling on POLYGON WOOD extremely heavy, causing many casualties. Lieuts. Boultbee & Phillis Hartman killed & Wallace wounded. L/Bn assisted Natural Barrage & ARTY. MSHT. defensive flank from J.10 c.6.0. in front of CAMERON HOUSE to J.N.a.3.4. Last attack died to date and reinforcements asked for. Enemy repeatedly attempted to advance but was driven back by our Lewis Gun and Rifle fire, and the line was held against further attacks. Touch with the S/Br Leicestershire Regt was maintained throughout on our left, the tack could not be kept with the troops on our right.	
		2.30 AM	Reinforcements from 4th Leicestershire Regt commenced to arrive, 2 Platoons sent up to reinforce front line and right flank. Enemy continued to shell extremely heavily particularly the W edge of POLYGON WOOD and GLENCORSE WOOD - BLACK WATCH CORNER Road. Two Coys of 4th Br Leicestershire Regt. who had suffered heavy casualties in the Barrage and were approximately 40 strong in all arrived as reinforcements.	

T2134. Wt. W708—776. 500000. 4/15. Sir J. C. & S.

Army Form C. 2118.

WAR DIARY
or
INTELLIGENCE SUMMARY.
(Erase heading not required.)

Instructions regarding War Diaries and Intelligence Summaries are contained in F. S. Regs., Part II. and the Staff Manual respectively. Title pages will be prepared in manuscript.

Place	Date	Hour	Summary of Events and Information	Remarks and references to Appendices
	Oct. 1st	10.30 a.m.	One Company sent to reinforce flank in T.10.c and one Coy sent to form a second line in T.10.B. central, 100 yards inside E edge of Poison Wood. Enemy shelling extremely heavy. Enemy aeroplane also appears on our enemy plane flying 200 feet above our trenches was shot down by our Richards and landed in "NO MAN'S LAND" where it was destroyed by our fire.	
		10.50 a.m.	No further enemy attack. Shelling still heavy. Many enemy wounded seen crawling out. Bret wounded. Enemy casualties appear to be very heavy.	
		12 noon	Major Hewitt O.C. 1st Leicesters Regt. arrived at Battn. H.Q. T.10.c.1.2. with one Coy of 1st Leicesters Regt. Major Hewitt took command of the situation. Enemy prisoners state that another attack will take place at dusk & all arrangements made accordingly. Consolidation and improvement of positions carried on throughout the afternoon. Movement extremely difficult on account of snipers and Machine Gun fire.	
		1.15 p.m.	Enemy again commenced to shell heavily but did not attack.	
		4.30 p.m.	Enemy reported by Lieut. Coy. to be massing in CAMERON COVERT and coming over ridge T.10.B. These parties were sickened by our fire.	

WAR DIARY
or
INTELLIGENCE SUMMARY.
(Erase heading not required.)

Army Form C. 2118.

Instructions regarding War Diaries and Intelligence Summaries are contained in F.S. Regs., Part II. and the Staff Manual respectively. Title pages will be prepared in manuscript.

Place	Date	Hour	Summary of Events and Information	Remarks and references to Appendices
	Oct 1st	5.30h	Enemy shelling increased	
		4.0h	S.O.S. from Bde. on our right. Our barrage came down about at once and continued for an hour. No enemy movement seen after our barrage stopped.	
		10.0pm	S.O.S. again reported on left and right. No enemy action on our front. Enemy fired showers of Very lights during our bombardment but did not shell heavily. Night passed comparatively quietly after the	
	Oct 2nd	5.30 AM	Protective barrage put down by our artillery when wounded any enemy attack. Our patrols active but no movement seen. They had the day our men had good shooting at enemy who attempted to run back from Shell holes. Enemy snipers apparently too	
		11.0h	S.O.S. reported on right at 7.15 p.m. but no action on our front. Batn. relieved by 9th K.O.Y.L.I. and moved back to Bank at Shortand Woop.	
	Oct 3	3.0 PM	Batn arrived in Camp in the Dickebush Area. Time spent in resting and reorganizing Batn.	
	Oct 4		Batn less Nucleus organised into two Coys. and amalgamated with	

WAR DIARY or INTELLIGENCE SUMMARY

Army Form C. 2118.

(Erase heading not required.)

Place	Date	Hour	Summary of Events and Information	Remarks and references to Appendices
	Oct 4th		The 8th Batt: which had also been organised into two Companies, joint Batt: dy-moving 99th Lancashire Regt: under command of Major Gatland & Lancashire Rgt. Batt. moved by Route March to Railway Dugouts area Z11.B.35.W.E.	
	Oct 5th	6.30pm	Batt. in RAILWAY DUGOUTS under direct orders of Division.	
			Batt. moved into forward Area. Two companies reoccupied trenches just East of POLYGON WOOD about J.10.c. central. The remaining two Coys went forward into close Support of the 7th Bn. Line Regt. who were holding this front line. Battalion in position without casualties by 10.15 pm.	
	" 6th	4.0 pm	Hostile Aeroplanes very active during the early morning. Boys were another intimation during morning and afternoon. Enemy & our artillery on to old trenches which we occupied shelling	
		4.45 pm	Weight of Barrage much heavier, particularly heavy just in front of trenches in J.10.c. and along Eastern edge of POLYGON WOOD.	
		4.53 pm	Our S.O.S. sent up all along front not in right up. Battalion took up battle positions. Lewis Guns were pushed forward and right flank along road, strengthened by Stafford Company	
		5.15pm	Hostile Barrage much less intense.	
		5.30pm	Situation quiet - Companies were withdrawn to normal positions Battalion placed under orders of 22nd Bde.	

Army Form C. 2118.

WAR DIARY
or
INTELLIGENCE SUMMARY.
(Erase heading not required.)

Instructions regarding War Diaries and Intelligence Summaries are contained in F. S. Regs., Part II. and the Staff Manual respectively. Title pages will be prepared in manuscript.

Place	Date	Hour	Summary of Events and Information	Remarks and references to Appendices
	Oct 8th		Two new Companies moved to new frontier area POLYGON BEEK into JON TREK TRENCH in J.10.d.	
	9th		Heavy shelling throughout the day - much difficulty in keeping up communication with rear.	
	10th		Battn. commenced to move back to camp in H.30.c. (ref Sheet 28) at 4.30 a.m. an enemy barrage Enemy opened a heavy fire on POLYGON WOOD which fell well short of part of the Battalion until dark.	
	11th		Battn. in Camp at H.30.c. by 4.40 a.m. Move by rail route to OUDERDOM at 12.30 pm when Battalion entrained and proceed to rest huts in BLARINGHEM AREA.	
	12th / 17th		9th Batt. moving to RACQUINGHEM and 8th Bn. to LE CROQUET. the 8/9th Batt. wheeled at E. BINGHEM. Battalion in rest at RACQUINGHEM. Reorganization and fine machine training carried out.	
	18th		Batt. moved by bus to Camp on Canadian Wood.	
	19th / 22nd		Bath. found working parties which took 90% of the men for R.E. Signals and Coys. work consisted of digging & filling in a cable trench. Hours 2-0 a.m. to 9.0 a.m.	
	23rd		Battn. moved to "C" Camp station dugout. H.30.c.3.2. Move complete by 1.37 p.m.	
	24th / 25th		Battn. in "C" Camp. Days spent in cleaning at bank, reorganising managing etc. Too wet to proceed with trench in a new part, part position on 25th. Brig. General commanding presented military medal ribbons to Pte 40 Pte L.M. Bn 6 m.g.	

D. D. & L. London, E. C.
(A8099) W. W1771/82-31 750,000 3/17 Sch.52 Forms/C2118/24

Army Form C. 2118.

WAR DIARY
or
INTELLIGENCE SUMMARY.
(Erase heading not required.)

Place	Date	Hour	Summary of Events and Information	Remarks and references to Appendices
	Oct 26		His Paxmton. Steven Proctor Smith M.O. who had joined us also during situation on October 14th.	
	" 27th		The Battn. moved into support, relieving 10th D.L.I. of 6th Bn. Relief complete without casualties.	
	" 28th		The Battn. relieved the 10th KOYLI on the left front-line sector. Lieut Alldritt wounded, 1 O.R. Killed ?- 4 O.R. Wounded.	
	" 29th		Shelling quiet during the morning, increasing in the afternoon.	
	" 30th		Hostile aeroplanes this morning, but our front line to early morning. Enemy shellfire very heavy during darkness. Intermittent shelling during the day, much quieter at night. Hostile aeroplanes again very active, continually flying low and using M.G.	
	" 31st		Battn. commenced to move back to reserve at ZILLEBEKE RAILWAY DUGOUTS at 4.30 pm. Relief very slow owing to Lorry Gas shell barrage between POLYGON WOODS and CHATEAU WOOD. Relieved by 8th LEIC. R.	
			Casualties during Month.	
			Killed 5 OR 50
			Wounded 7 213
			Missing - 36
			Lost 12 301

R.M. Matland Major
8th (?) Leic R.

WAR DIARY or INTELLIGENCE SUMMARY

Army Form C. 2118.

9th Leicestershire Regt.

Place	Date 1917	Hour	Summary of Events and Information	Remarks and references to Appendices
	Nov 1st Nov 2nd Nov 3rd-6th Nov 7th Nov 8th		Batt. was in Billets at Railway Dugouts, Zillebeke Lake. Batt. moved up Reserve at C'teau. CHATEAU SEGARD. B. remained in Reserve until 8th inst. Batt. moved to Brigade Reserve at ZILLEBEKE (Inhay Dugouts). Batt. moved up to the line. Relieved the 16th Bn. of R. Left Brigade (1st R.A.K.R.L.) Relief was completed by 10 P.M. Reconnoitred enemy outposts. Several enemy position - B.Z.9 in front line - B.Z.9 in Support; BUTTE (Bn. HQrs.) to front line at 6.15 AM. Enemy place was mounted of fallen Pillbox etc., in a spot N. of TOURNEL WOOD at 3 0 P.M. Enemy Pill ... Support line 5 in low timber ... appeared jealous. - J.7.I.A.6.6.9 J.7.2.A.O.5.6.O. (approx West) J.5.4.5.3) Enemy Pill boxes located at LOVIE X ROADS which front line attacked about 12.30 P.M. Artillery bombarded Tournel Wood	
	Nov 9th		at 6.00 A.M. 1.30 A.M. & 4.30 P.M. Enemy Patrol, all normal strength, left TOURNAL WOOD and J.12.0.0.7) & came N.N.W. direction. Some of our Lewis Gun Posts ...	
	Nov 10th & 12th		moved at ... our Patrol to get within 30 yds. of the Lewis Gun fired five. The Patrol was scattered & our Lewis Gun'd fired TOURNAL WOOD. Casualties could not be counted were Patrol returned.	
	Nov 13th Nov 14th Nov 15th Nov 16th Nov 17th Nov 18th Nov 19th		On the night of 12/13th Batt. was relieved by 6th Bn. Lec. Regt. & moved back to Brigade Support by Railway Dugouts ZILLEBEKE. B. Coy. remaining at POLYGON BUTTE, at the disposal of 27th Bde. Capt. Batt. moved to FORESTER CAMP & remained over night. B. Coy. was relieved by 11th Bn. BUTTE & moved back joining the Batt. at 11.15 P.M. Whole Batt. was carried out by Buses, taken. Batt. proceeded by train to Road to TRENFINOR COMB.REMINGHURST. Coy. Lorries was carried out. Batt. proceeded by Entrained at LA BECOQUE. Batt. proceeded by Entrained to PT. Mad LA BECOQUE. to Pt. M de BOIS

Army Form C. 2118.

WAR DIARY
or
INTELLIGENCE SUMMARY
(Erase heading not required.)

Instructions regarding War Diaries and Intelligence Summaries are contained in F. S. Regs., Part II. and the Staff Manual respectively. Title Pages will be prepared in manuscript.

Place	Date	Hour	Summary of Events and Information	Remarks and references to Appendices
	Nov 20th		Batt. proceeded by route march to MT PEMMENCHON	
	Nov 21st		Batt. proceeded by route march to HERBIN	
	Nov 22nd		N.C.Os were billeted in billets by large numbers, being extensively used getting 3 derived kits in the field (The NUNNERY). Casualties 7 killed, 4 died of wounds. (3 of the latter died of wounds n. 22.9).	
	Nov 23rd		Four of the men killed were buried with full Military Honours.	
	Nov 24th		Batt. remained in same billets at CAPRIN	
	Nov 25th		Most Training and carried out under Company arrangements.	
	Nov 26th & 30th		Batt. marched to XIII Corps Training Area, once billeted at MAGNICOURT-LE-COMTE. Batn. carried out Training.	

Casualties during month
KILLED Officers — O.R. 12
WOUNDED 12 41
MISSING — 1
            — —
            2 54

AMcLeum Lt acting for Lieut-Colonel
Comdg 9th Leicestershire Regt.

WAR DIARY or INTELLIGENCE SUMMARY

Army Form C. 2118.

9th Leicestly Regt

Dec 1917

29.C
2 sheets

Place	Date	Hour	Summary of Events and Information	Remarks and references to Appendices
	1st			
	2nd		Battalion arrived TINCOURT Station at 10.0 pm, having been ordered to entrain at SAXY STATION by 9.0 pm on 30.1 Nov. Battalion was ordered to proceed to the line and take over trenches E. of EPEHY. Relief complete without casualties	
	3rd		New line thoroughly reconnoitred, front strongpoints &c. No enemy activity. Enemy wounding & quiet. Positions consolidated &c.	
	4th			
	5th		Battn was relieved by 8th Bn Leicesters Regt in the trenches and marched back to PRONNE KILLED at VILLERS FAUCON. Relief complete by 8.30 pm without casualties.	
	6th		Battalion in rest, cleaning up &c.	
	7th			
	8th		Bn relieved the 8th Bn Leic Regt in same trench sector. Relief commenced 5.33 pm and completed without casualties by 6.39 pm.	
	9th		Actual enemy activity on Battalion front. Nil. The enemy occasionally shells the Village of EPEHY.	
	10th		Enemy Artillery activity very lively, for this sector. CATELET VALLEY being shelled from 9.0 am onwards with all calibre.	
	11th		Yesterday shots not repeated. Shells occurring on its usual shelf of Park	
	12th		Bttn MOVED to EPEHY from 10.0 am onwards. Battalion now relieved by R.I.R. 16. Garrison and moved into B SUPPORT in EPEHY.	
	13th		Work on Village line & defences.	
	15th			
	16th		Bttn relieve 5th Bn R.E. Regt in 9th Divnl Sector front Saturday from X.26.a.3.5	

WAR DIARY
or
INTELLIGENCE SUMMARY
(Erase heading not required.)

Army Form C. 2118.

Place	Date	Hour	Summary of Events and Information	Remarks and references to Appendices
	17th		Enemy activity normal. We carried out very active patrolling	
	18th		Intermittent enemy shelling with 7.7 mm guns in between front & support trenches to be at X.27.B. Enemy front line reported to be one of our posts.	
	19th		10 of the enemy were observed on PARRS LANE, they were dispersed by M.G. fire.	
	20th		Battalion relieved by 8th Bn. Leic Rgt. and moved into RESERVE at SAILLECOURT	
	21st			
	22nd		Battalion in rest	
	23rd		Christmas dinner on 23rd	
	24th		Battalion relieved the 8th Bn. Leic Rgt. in the trenches	
	25th			
	26th		Very little activity on part of the enemy. Batt. relieved by 8 Bn. Leic Rt.	
	30th		and moved into support on 25th inst.	
	31st		Work on the village defences proceeded with.	

Casualties Henry Thomas

KILLED	WOUNDED
2	5

OTHER RANKS

H Hewn ? Major
for O.C. 9th Leic Bn.

WAR DIARY
INTELLIGENCE SUMMARY

Army Form C. 2118.

9th Bn. Royal Fusiliers Regt.

January 1918

Place	Date	Hour	Summary of Events and Information	Remarks
	1918 Jan 1		Batt relieved the 8th Batt Lincolnshire Regt in Bgde 2nd Resn. Relief complete by 7.30 pm	
	2nd		Artillery/Trench Mortars Normal. Machine Guns (Woods) shot turns heavy with opportunity to keep guns warm. T.O.A in trench nearly unperceived owing to deep trench MUD.	
	3rd		Artillery (Hostile) Normal enemy guns active 6.30 pm & 11 pm, on road JUNCTION M.4.d.7. Trench life fairly in and informed.	
	4th		Batt relieved by 10th Batt ROYAL FUSILIERS today except for rear Platn at LONGAVESNES & reserve Platn. Batt relieved 10.30 am	
	5th, 6th, 7th		Time spent at LONGAVESNES cleaning up, inspections. By Brigr Hardie Bull today	
	10th & 11th		Batt marched to LONGAVESNES & HAUT ALLAINES arrived in Camp Night 12.30 am. Time at HAUT ALLAINES by Heavy (Welcome Bombs). Firing Bombs (rough range). During the march billets over & Bgde by Right Genes C.B also beaten by Bgde D. E. Mayby MA. & officers of the Regn in Trench Master.	
	30		Batt moved from HAUT ALLAINES by light railway to SOMECOURT for training. At M.o.J.4.4	

WAR DIARY
or
INTELLIGENCE SUMMARY.
(Erase heading not required.)

Army Form C. 2118.

Place	Date	Hour	Summary of Events and Information	Remarks and references to Appendices
	1915 Jan 20 to Jan 24		Batt. in RESERVE at SAILLY COURT. Troops down to Baths by Thursday & washing & refitting. The nights of the Batt. marched up from SAILLY COURT & relieved 8th Royal East Kents in Right Sub Sector.	
	25		Artillery machine gun (hostile) & our own MG harrassed.	
	26		Artillery (ours) very active in silencing hostile EPEHY	
	27		Batt. Front very quiet Fog & mist all day. We had slight contact with the enemy but no great infantry activity. 3 Platoons of Z.C.O. to the M.S. South Sector. & 1 platoon of a Coy to T.S.C.	
	28		Quiet on Batt. front. EA & our own arty. active during day. Quiet night. Batt. relieved by 3rd Batt. LEICESTERSHIRE R. at 6:30pm & moved to the village EPEHY	
	29 30 31		Batt. in EPEHY. Time spent in washing & refitting. Supper Pros. Carriers' running dumps.	

O.R. MILES Officer of Regiment (Name ...)
+
R. McFarland Lt. Col. Commanding 9th Batt. Leicestershire Regt.

Army Form C. 2118.

WAR DIARY
or
INTELLIGENCE SUMMARY.
(Erase heading not required.)

9th Leicestershire Regt   Vol 31

Place	Date	Hour	Summary of Events and Information	Remarks and references to Appendices
	1/9/18		Batt. relieve the 8th Batt Leicestershire Regt in Bgde Res, Relief complete by 7.45 pm front of EPEHY.	
	2/9/18		Batt front very quiet.	
	3/9/18		do do do	
	4/9/18	9 pm	do do Batt relieved by 8th Batt Leicestershire By. & moved into Reserve at SAULCOURT CAMP. Batt arrived in camp at 9 pm	
	5/9/18		Batt in Reserve at SAULCOURT	
	6/9/18		Batt in Reserve at SAULCOURT	
	7/9/18	3 pm	Batt moved from SAULCOURT to MOISLAINS by light railway at 5.30 pm arrived in camp, MOISLAINS at 5.30 pm	
	8/9/18		Draft of 9 Officers & 198 Other Ranks Left by bus to join Bn Batt Leicestershire Regt. near BAPAUME.	
	9/9/18		Staff conducted to D.H. Officer & men & DADOS Talks prepared and Drafts arranged for B.Q.M.S. Batt Lieutenant Col to men & practised at 9 am by Officers & practised at 9 am by Officers	
	7/9/18		Lecture 1/ 3 Officers & 60 O.R prepared at 9 am & practised Batt. Lieut Colonel By at HUT ALLAINS by march route by march route by Baren	

Army Form C. 2118

WAR DIARY
or
INTELLIGENCE SUMMARY.
(Erase heading not required.)

Instructions regarding War Diaries and Intelligence Summaries are contained in F. S. Regs., Part II. and the Staff Manual respectively. Title pages will be prepared in manuscript.

Place	Date	Hour	Summary of Events and Information	Remarks and references to Appendices
	10/2/18		Draft of 11 officers & 240 O.R. proceeded at 2 p.m. in fourteens to join 7th Batt. West Yorkshire Regt. at MOISLAINS	
	11/2/18		10.10 German prisoners etc handed over to D.D.D.S.	
			Draft of 14 officers & 236 O.R. proceeded at 9 am to proceed to join 2nd Batt. Lincolnshire Regt. at YORK CAMP. MOISLAINS	
	12/2/18		Reports in respect of Officers & O.R. received opposite sent from the Bn.	
			Remainder of men handed over to D.D.D.S.	
	13/2/18		Bath of N.C.O's & privates & spare kit sent up at HUT HUPPINS.	
	14/2/18 to 20/2/18		HQ's continued to send out details at Eblant Encampment	

20.2.18.

M.W. Yeomans. Lt. Col.
Comdg. 9th (S) Batt. The Lincolnshire Regt.

www.ingramcontent.com/pod-product-compliance
Lightning Source LLC
Chambersburg PA
CBHW081557160426
43191CB00011B/1954